New-Founde-Land

*at
the Very Centre
of the European Discovery &
Exploration of North America.*

R.H. Cuff

Cover design by Hilary Cass.

Book Design by Kathy Hudson.

Dedicated to Alex, Sefora, and Harry.

The Johnson Family Foundation and the author wish to express their appreciation to Dr. Leslie Harris for reviewing drafts of this work.

ISBN 1-896338-12-7

Printed by:
Robinson Blackmore Printing and Publishing Ltd., St. John's.

Published by:
Harry Cuff Publications Limited
94 LeMarchant Rd.
St. John's, Nfld.
A1C 2H2

New-Founde-Land

1.

"To adventure as becometh men".

New-Founde-Land waters as the cradle of Discovery.

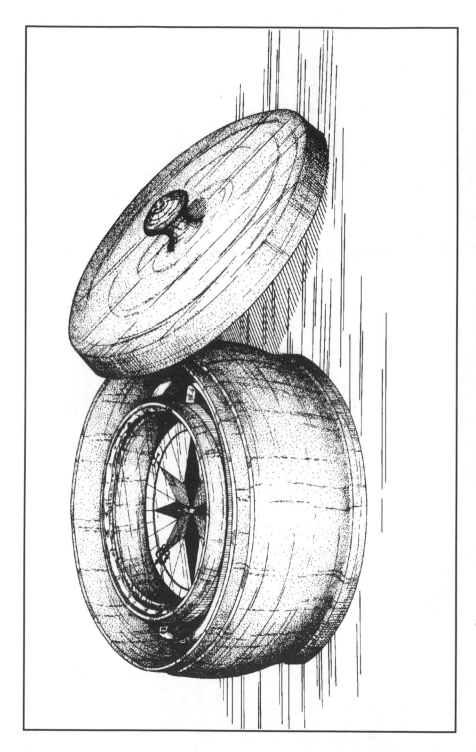

Compass and case reconstruction. (Drawing by Carol Pillar, courtesy Parks Canada.)

This book, researched and written as the 1997 Cabot Anniversary approached, serves to emphasize the little-recognized fact that the New-Founde-Land, or Terra Nova, was at the epicentre of the entire era of European exploration of North America. For roughly a century, between 1497 and the first efforts to settle the new land in 1610, more than a dozen well-known explorers from England, France, Spain, and Portugal set their sails for the waters of the New-Founde-Land.

Given the Island's key geographic position — hundreds of miles closer to Europe than any other part of the continent — Newfoundland became the gateway to North America. The Sixteenth Century was not the only era to find the New-Founde-Land at midstream in the currents of progress. The first transatlantic telegraph cables, the first wireless telegraphy, the pioneering transatlantic flights, and the first intercontinental air terminals — all relied upon this strategically important island.

This story about the discovery and exploration of the New-Founde-Land is an epic tale, replete with forceful and colourful personalities, unsolved mysteries, tragic errors in judgement, battles against the forces of nature, and the tremendous courage and determination to realize a vision, against all the odds.

Late in the spring of 1497, an Italian-born master navigator, Giovanni Caboto, made a 35-day crossing of the Atlantic out from the port of Bristol, England. Sailing under the authority of letters patent from the English King Henry VII and financed by a company of Bristol adventurers, Caboto was attempting to reach Japan and establish trade with China. He had an English ship and a largely Bristolian crew — who knew him as John Cabot.

On his return to England, about 80 days after embarking, Cabot's proclamation of his achievement began the 100 years in which our island was like a ship moored right in the midst of all the adventuresome voyages. Indeed, the names ''New-Founde-Land'' and ''Terra Nova'' were originally applied by Europeans to the whole of North America as it was then known. In the early 1500s, virtually all European knowledge of North America was centred around the New-Found-Land and, accordingly, each navigator setting out for the New World made straight for our waters. Only later did ''Newfoundland'' apply only to this island, when Jacques

Cartier's explorations of the Gulf of St. Lawrence proved it to be separate from the mainland.

It was a full century later before the eastern seaboard of North America became known to kings and court cartographers, and before transatlantic mariners would abandon their customary practice of sailing first for Newfoundland waters. For 100 years and more, the first sign that the Ocean crossing had been achieved was coming into

A late 15th-century ship heaving the lead upon entering the English Channel. (Courtesy Parks Canada.)

soundings on the Grand Banks — when the lead-line was able to make bottom for the first time in a month or even two.

Samuel de Champlain, the founder of the Quebec colony, made some 21 Atlantic crossings in the early 1600s and the journal of his first voyage, in May of 1603, notes a typical first impression of North America. After coming into soundings ''upon the Bank, where the fishing is carried on'' in latitude 44°20', Champlain's first sight of what is now Canada, came four days later:

> *On the sixth of the said month, we came so near land that we heard the sea beat against the shore, but could not see it for the thickness of the fog, to which these coasts are subject; and on this account we again put out to sea some leagues, until the weather being very clear, we sighted land, which was Cape St. Mary's.*

Some scholars have suggested that a ''new isle'' was already known in Bristol, before Cabot's voyage of 1497. Yet, it was certainly not until the 1490s that rumours of new discoveries overseas were publicized outside of a closed-fraternity of master navigators and/or merchant adventurers of Bristol — and were eventually communicated with some urgency to the crowned heads of Europe. If the discovery of a New Isle during John Cabot's voyage of 1497 was really something of a surprise, his voyage the following year took place against a backdrop of mounting excitement about the New-Founde-Land beyond the seas.

In June and July of 1497, as John Cabot saw a bewildering procession of capes and islands parade from behind the curtain of the unknown, one wonders, what did he believe he had found? It seems clear that Cabot was more open-minded as to the shape of the New World than was Christopher Columbus. Columbus went to his grave still protesting that he had reached Asia, in the face of mounting evidence that his ''Indies'' were nothing of the sort. John Cabot seems to have believed from the first that his was a true ''first discovery'' of a *new* land to the north of the country of the Great Khan. But, if John Cabot were able to accept that he had failed in his goal of reaching the wealthy kingdom of Cipango (Japan), he still hoped that the New-Founde-Land would prove to be a way-station which would allow England access to the riches of the Orient.

Following the events of 1497, it was in the 1500's that the largely unexplored Atlantic Ocean ceased to be a barrier for Europeans and became, gradually, a starting place rather than an end. It was a time when changes in navigation and map-making were opening up a new world, which literally changed from day to day. And, the strategic position of the New-Founde-Land, between the New World and the Old, was of utmost significance and importance.

This book has been produced lest we should forget, in this Cabot 500th Anniversary Year, that the voyage of John Cabot in the *Matthew* was but one event, in the dawning of an important era in the history of the western world. The New-Founde-Land was truly the cradle, not only of British and French overseas trade, but of the British Empire, of Canada, and of the United States of America.

*   *   *

Edward Hayes sailed to the New-Founde-Land with Sir Humphrey Gilbert in 1583, only to see the expedition's leader ''devoured and swallowed up by the sea'' on the return voyage. Captain Hayes still believed that ''it were better to adventure as becometh men... [than] very miserably to live and die... in a country pestered with inhabitants.'' And, there are those of us today, pestered to distraction in our ''global village,'' who see the Age of Discovery as a romantic era, in which man courageously pursued the unknown, for the sake of adventure and great reward.

Others, who see so much new knowledge in our satellite-imaged world, may snicker at John Cabot and his contemporaries, who persisted in attempts to reach Asia by sailing to the west. But we should consider that John Cabot's adopted city-state of Venice had thrived and prospered, based on the trade in spices and other exotic goods from Asia. Cabot, Christopher Columbus, Gaspar Corte Real and Giovanni da Verrazzano were not mere adventurers-for-hire, but were lured — as are the pioneers of our own time — by the knowledge that profit and renown are associated first-and-foremost with risk. Even in 1497, the lure of venturing into the unknown and finding great riches were the driving impetus for great boldness.

Indeed, given the rigid social structure of Europe in the 1500s, explorations which might add new dominions for the sovereign were one avenue which held exciting potential for master mariners. With marketable skills, but of humble birth and modest means, they had access to the patronage of the crown. Cabot embarked, not only to add new lands to Henry VII's realm, but in the hope of becoming "known to fame" and being granted estates and perhaps a title of nobility to be passed down to his sons.

In the first instance, the New-Founde-Land was discovered by accident. The second round of exploration concentrated, in essence, on looking for a way around this new land — while coincidentally "discovering" the coast. Once it had been established by the early voyages, that neither the "Indies" nor the "New-Founde-Land" were parts of Asia, the focus for further voyages was, in the words of Sebastian Cabot, "to go by the north to Cathay, and bring thence spices in a shorter time than the Portuguese did by the south." In the 1500s, these efforts set out the very boundaries of the known world, the New-Founde-Land.

*   *   *

Exactly how much profit was felt to be at stake in the quest for a shorter route to the Orient? What vision of riches created the Age of Discovery and gave rise to the quests of Cabot, Columbus, and so many others? Leaving aside for the moment the boundless hoards of fancy, let us consider the actual potential of the trade in spices.

In 1519, Ferdinand Magellan, a Portuguese, sailing in the employ of the Spanish, embarked on a voyage to the Orient via the west. This expedition has since become well-known as the first circumnavigation of the globe — but came close to obliteration. Magellan started out with five ships, and a complement of 270 men, supplied by the King of Spain. He was provisioned for two years, including arms, ammunition, and a great quantity of goods to trade. Most readers may be aware of the dreadful hardships endured over the course of Magellan's epic voyage. It lasted three years and suffered many losses, including the lives of Magellan himself, and all but 14 men, and all but one of the ships. Yet the one ship that did return, the *Vittoria*, had secured a cargo of cloves in the Moluccas —

and which amazingly was valuable enough to actually cover the entire costs of the expedition!

Later in the century, a second celebrated voyage around the world by the Englishman Francis Drake took two years, but realized a profit of 4700%. The major "adventurer" (investor), Queen Elizabeth I, realized a profit of £160,000 — something approaching $250,000,000 in today's money. Drake himself was rewarded with a knighthood, popular adulation, a captain's share of the voyage, and the assurance that further expeditions would find ready financial support from "merchant adventurers".

The mariners whose lives and explorations are chronicled here generally were not fully supported by the state. But, neither were they mercenaries, simply offering the purported "secrets of the east" to the highest bidder. (Sebastian Cabot, son-of-John, was perhaps, the exception which proves the rule). The course followed by Cabot-the-father was more typical. The Italian-born Cabot had a grandiose idea of a northern route to Asia, via the "islands in the Ocean Sea" and Japan, but he was without the private means to undertake such a voyage. As a man with a vision who was not a member of the elite, he had attempted to interest the crowns of Spain and Portugal in his enterprise, without success.

A royal charter, if not the financial backing of the monarch, was crucial, if an expedition was to reap the rewards in terms of titles or prestige that were expected — and which Cabot would certainly feel he was entitled to, as vindication for the years in which he had been trying to promote his vision. Thus, Cabot's letters patent from Henry VII entitled him to possess and govern such New Lands as he might discover, much as the Corte Reals were to be granted the "captaincy" of new lands they might discover.

While Cabot's charter specified that Henry VII was to have "the fifth part of the capital gain so gotten for every then voyage," the voyage was not in any way financed by either the state or from the King's privy purse — but rather fell "upon [Cabot's] own proper costs and charges." Later, once the new lands were known to exist, royal investment was forthcoming. Generally, the small sums invested by the English crown did not suggest that the discovery of new lands was considered a great affair of state by King Henry.

Fortunately, the early explorers were able to draw upon the "merchant adventurers" — investors who were enlisted in support of most voyages, before political approaches were made. For instance, John Cabot is known to have had the backing of the merchant adventurers of the port of Bristol. Giovanni da Verrazzano had assembled a syndicate of Dieppe shipowners, and some silk merchants of Lyons.

Certainly sometimes an explorer's second voyage found the support of the Crown less grudging. For Cabot's second voyage Henry VII supplied and equipped one of the four ships from the royal coffers. The pattern seems to have been new lands being discovered by a single ship or small expedition, followed by high hopes and increased royal patronage — followed, in many instances, by disaster.

If their motives varied at the outset, virtually all of the explorers chronicled herein returned from their initial voyages glassy-eyed with the prospects of further exploration and the potential of the New-Founde-Land. They were encouraged, and determined, as John Davis wrote at the end of his second voyage in 1587, "to see an end of these businesses." In Davis's case he was even willing to sell his portion of the family estate in order to continue exploring, although he and his adventurers attempted to ensure meeting their commitments by outfitting two of the expedition's three ships to engage in the fishery.

It was the assurance of backing for further voyages, and the prospect of expeditions of trade or conquest, that were the most tangible rewards for the successful explorer. There were assuredly personal rewards as well — such as Cabot's £10 "to hym that founde the new Isle" and his £20 pension after his first voyage, and Jacques Cartier's prize of the ship *Grand Hermine* after his second. But, the major gain was royal backing for follow up voyages. Thus, for Cabot's second voyage, the English King himself supplied and equipped a ship.

Royal patronage also encouraged London merchants to become involved in the adventure. After his first voyage "on his own account, and at his own expense," Gaspar Corte Real seems to have had his three caravels in 1501 supplied by King Manoel of Portugal.

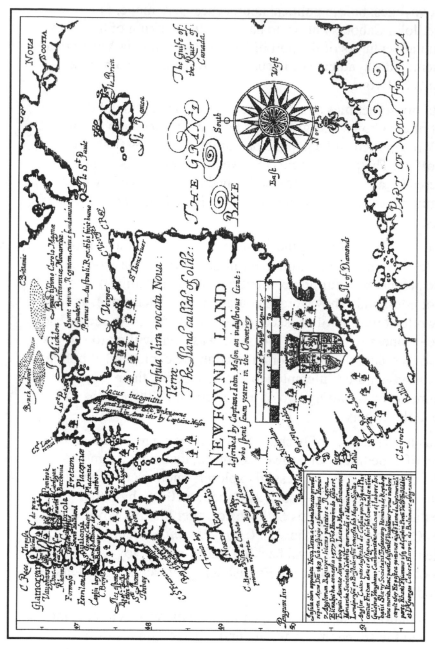

"The lland called of olde Newfound Land," a map by Governor John Mason of the Cuper's Cove colony. By the time this first English map of Newfoundland was published in 1625, the name was already "olde," having a long cartographical history. It was Mason who identified Cape Bonavista as the land "first seen by Cabot". (Courtesy Harry Cuff Publications.)

In 1524 Giovanni da Verrazzano was assured by François I, of France, of continued royal patronage, to further explore his discoveries — although this promise fell through, due to circumstance and politics. François I later outfitted Jacques Cartier's first voyage, rewarding the Breton navigator after its completion with a new commission and increased Royal support.

It was the French who began seriously exploring the region, while they were chiefly searching for the ephemeral kingdoms of Norumbega and Saguenay. Bearing in mind the Spanish bonanza in central America, François I still held out hopes that New France might yield an Indian prince, civilized enough to have accumulated a horde of gold or other riches — for trade, or even for conquest.

Most of the famed explorers either died while on their voyages (including John Cabot, the Corte Reals, Verrazzano, Davis, and Hudson) or, like Jacques Cartier, lost royal favour and retreated into the obscurity from which they had emerged. Nonetheless, most are better known to history than the kings and queens in whose service they sailed.

Try as they might, the early explorers simply could not make the New-Founde-Land serve for Japan, or use Terra Nova as a way station en route to the Orient. The dawning of this fact was a severe disappointment.

After an entire century of North American discovery, Martin Frobisher was able to say of the Northwest Passage "it is still the only thing left undone, whereby a notable mind might be made famous and remarkable." The eighth chapter of this book deals with a series of explorations, intent on finding some passage through what was, by then, recognized to be a continent. These ambitions were bound (we now know) to lead to disappointment. Chapter eight also deals with the period in which Elizabethan England, captivated by the romance of seamanship, asserted her control over New-Founde-Land waters against the Spanish and Portuguese — leaving France as her only serious and determined rival for North America.

Despite a century of frustrated ambitions, and while the New-Founde-Land was not the island that John Cabot had envisioned as Cipangu, or the Island of the Seven Cities, it did become the prime destination across the Ocean Sea. This island served as a landmark and staging ground from which to explore and exploit a vast and rich land, North America, on the other side. Indeed, England and France continued to battle over the waters and coasts of Newfoundland in a seemingly endless struggle, which continued for three hundred years after Cabot's voyage. But that is another story.

"The manner of Fishing ... at New Found Land," from a map cartouche by Herman Moll, 1710.

2.

St. Brendan, 565 to 572 AD.

The Norse, 986 to 1011 AD.

*"The Land of Promise of the Saints" &
"Vinland the Good".*

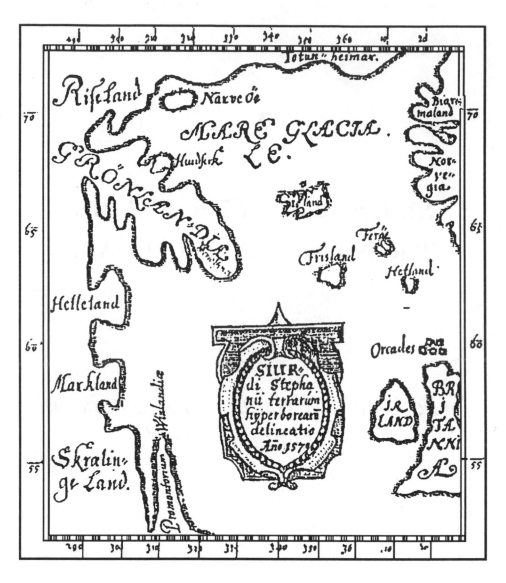

This map, drawn by Icelandic schoolmaster Sigurdur Steffansson in 1570, shows Greenland, Helluland, Markland, and Skraelingland. Promonterium Winlandia (Vinland Peninsula) is obviously the Great Northern Peninsula of Newfoundland. (Photo: the Royal Library, Copenhagen.)

The first attempt by Europeans to colonize North America was conducted between about AD1000 and 1020, by a couple of hundred Norse men and women — the people known in popular folklore as "Vikings". "Viking" is a poor term for the first Europeans who attempted to settle Newfoundland. Among the Northmen, to go viking meant a particular trade or profession of the warrior-elite, involving piracy, trade and land-taking. Viking is particularly associated with a period in which the Norse people wrought havoc and subsequently settled much of northern Europe and the British Isles, between about AD 800 and 1070. The notion of bloodthirsty raiders interferes with an understanding of the history of the handful of Norse farmers who achieved a brief foothold in North America, only to be driven out of the new country by "Skraelings" wielding arrows and spears with stone points.

While nearly three centuries of Norse expansion were marked by viking raids and war, this was also a time of increased trade in the northeast Atlantic and of colonization by Norse landholders, few of whom belonged to the fierce warrior elite. There is every indication that in Newfoundland, the Greenland Norse sought pasture for their sheep and cattle — and trade goods such as timber — rather than piracy and conquest. In fact, part of the initial attraction of "Vinland" was that it appeared to be uninhabited. The other North Atlantic islands that the Norse had settled over the preceding 200 years (Greenland and Iceland) had, originally, been uninhabited as well.

The chief documents concerning the Norse attempts to settle Newfoundland and Labrador are two Icelandic sagas: the *Greenlanders Saga* and *Eiriks Saga*. As the sagas were not written down until about 200 years after the events they describe, it is perhaps not surprising that scholars were, and are, at odds as to how to interpret them. For instance: how literally can one rely upon such evidence as sailing times and geographic details in the two sagas? They were handed down by word-of-mouth or recitation over many generations before being committed to parchment. Since the 1960s, and the discovery of the remainder of a Norse settlement at L'Anse aux Meadows at the northernmost tip of Newfoundland, some of the Norse traditions of "Vinland" (as recorded in the *Sagas*) have been substantiated by archaeology.

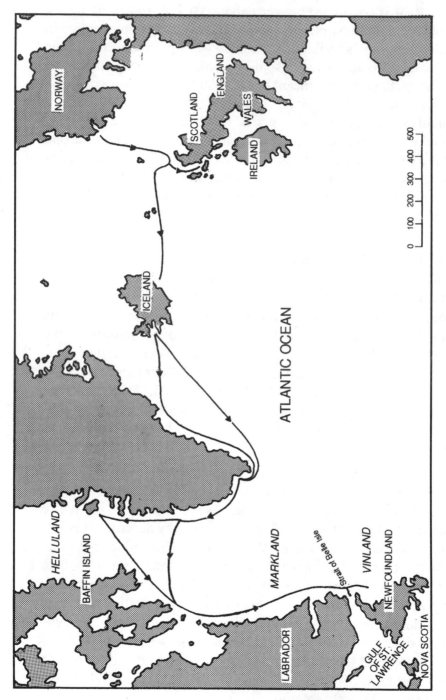

The Norse voyages in the North Atlantic, from Norway to Vinland. (Map by Kathy Hudson).

There have been many suggestions that there was some contact between the New World and the Old before the voyages of Christopher Columbus and John Cabot in the 1490s. Of these, amongst the most intriguing are the few shreds of evidence which suggest that seafaring Irish monks reached the New World at some time between the mid-500s and about AD 700. The Irish tales of such voyages are even more entangled with myth and fantasy than the Norse *Sagas*. To date there is no archaeological or historical evidence to support an Irish discovery of North America. The Irish tradition of voyaging is still worth considering, if only because it provides a context in which to place the Norse expansion in the north Atlantic.

After about AD 400 and the work of St. Patrick in Christianizing that island country, Ireland was a stronghold of learning and culture in the British Isles. By the 600s, Irish monks had been voyaging to the north for many years in ox-hide boats (*curraghs*) and had established isolated monasteries on uninhabited islands to the north of Britain — the Hebrides, Orkneys, Shetlands and Faeroes (the last being reached in about 700). By tradition, the widest-ranging of the Irish monks was St. Brendan. The Voyage of St. Brendan is said to have lasted seven years, from about 565 to 572.

St. Brendan was certainly a real person, one who was much travelled and one who was important in the early history of the Irish church. Yet accounts of St. Brendan as a hero, which began to be recorded in about 900, are considered likely to be a mythological account or "pious fable" romanticizing the entire era of exploration by Irish monks. Few would maintain that the *Navigatio Sancti Brendani* is a literal account of one voyage in search of Paradise. Rather, the Voyage of St. Brendan, as recorded in the tenth century, is a series of adventures much of which is demonstrably fictional.

Brendan and his party are said to have visited many Atlantic islands, eventually reaching a vast country which they explored for 40 days. Many of the events and islands described in the voyage are fantastic, bordering on the bizarre — including encounters with Judas Iscariot, birds who sang the Latin mass and a friendly whale named Jasconius (see plate II). Yet, some descriptive passages are taken to indicate an Irish knowledge (at the very least by the time that the tradition of the voyage was recorded) of Iceland and the waters around Greenland. There are also tantalizing hints about a land further to the west.

While few would go so far as to equate St. Brendan's "Land of Promise of the Saints" with either North America in general or Newfoundland in particular, the remarkable sea voyages of the Irish monks in their ox-hide curraghs show that no definite limits can be placed on their possible exploits. It was certainly the Irish who opened the eyes of the Norse to the possibility that there were virgin lands, occupied only by religious solitaries, to the north and west of Britain.

In the 800s, Norse sea raiders were a dreaded sight along the coasts of Britain and Ireland. The earliest of these raids were conducted against isolated and undefended seaside monasteries. While there was perhaps little profit in raiding Irish hermit monks, the attacks of the raiders led the Irish to abandon the northern islands. The Norse soon had knowledge of the islands north of Scotland, and their farmers who came in later years established settlements.

In about 860, a Norse trader was driven out to sea by a storm and came within sight of Iceland. Soon there was talk of settling this remote island. From 870 to 930, the best grazing lands in Iceland were occupied. The Norse sagas briefly confirm for us that the first Norse settlers found a scattering of Irish *papars* (probably from the Latin *papa*, for priest or monk), who quickly left Iceland.

By 930, the habitable areas of Iceland had been settled by about 30,000 Norse when rumours began to circulate of yet another land to the west, again discovered by a storm-driven trader. Yet it was another 50 years before anyone attempted to explore this new land. The exploration was proposed by a Norse resident of Iceland who had recently arrived from Norway — Eirik *raudi* (or Eric the Red).

Eirik's career would seem to provide evidence that the viking tradition was not entirely dead among the Norse by the late 900s. He had come to Iceland after being banished from Norway "because of some killings", but soon was engaged in another blood feud and was driven to a more remote area of Iceland. There he killed Eyjolf Saur and Hrafn "the Dueller" and was banished from Iceland for three years.

Being unwelcome in Norway, and perhaps tiring of neighbours and feuds, Eirik decided to explore the land reported to lie to the west. He did so in a three-year voyage, and named the land Greenland, for "people would be more tempted to go there if it had an attractive name". He noted places for farms, including his own at Eiriksfjord. When his banishment expired, Eirik returned to Iceland and spent a winter enrolling colonists. He eventually found 400 to make the trip (for land-pressure was beginning to be felt in Iceland) and set out. This was probably the year 985 or 986. Of 25 vessels which set out west from the Snaefells Glacier, only 14 made it to Eiriksfjord. The rest were either lost or returned to Iceland. The Icelanders began to establish farms in the area, which became known as *Eystribygden* (the "Eastern Settlement").

After exploring much of the vast Greenland coast, the places that Eirik had chosen were fiords north and west of what is now Cape Farewell (Greenland's southernmost tip). The majority of the

Reconstructed Norse sod huts at L'Anse aux Meadows. (Courtesy Parks Canada.)

colonists settled around Eiriksfjord and nearby Einarsfjord, but there were more isolated farmsteads as well, including (possibly in later years), a second settlement well to the northwest. This was *Vestribygden* or the "Western Settlement". The farmstead nearest Cape Farewell was taken up by Herjolf Bardarson, one of the first wave of settlers, and became known as Herjolfness.

Shortly after Herjolf had sailed to Greenland, his son Bjarni returned to Iceland from a trading voyage to Norway. Although he had no experience of the crossing to Greenland, Bjarni quickly determined to follow his father and his crew were persuaded to make the voyage as well. Beset by storms and fog, Bjarni's vessel was carried well west of his intended course and, being unable to see the sun for days on end, he soon lost his bearings. Eventually they came to a well-forested coast, which Bjarni knew from what he had heard could not be Greenland. He turned to the north, and coasted the country for five days, although he did not land. He eventually reached Greenland.

Although Bjarni Herjolfsson chose to give up voyaging and farm with his father, the *Greenlanders Saga* notes that "there was now great talk of discovering new countries". Once the earliest pioneering days had passed in Greenland, the wanderlust began to emerge again, particularly among the family of Eirik the Red. In about 1000 or 1001 (that is, approximately 15 years after the settling of Greenland and Bjarni's accidental discovery), Leif Eiriksson went to see Bjarni at Herjolfness, bought Bjarni's ship and engaged 35 men for a voyage of discovery.

Eirik originally agreed to lead the expedition himself, but declined to do so after falling from a horse as the vessel prepared to depart. (Not only was he injured, but this fall was regarded as a particularly bad omen.) After leaving Greenland and sailing west, Leif reached a land with glaciers and no grass, the land between the glaciers and the shoreline "like one great slab of rock". This was probably Baffin Island or northernmost Labrador. Having gone one better than Bjarni by actually landing, Leif decided to name the country Helluland ("slab" or "flat stone land"). Further south, he coasted a flat country with sandy beaches and a well-wooded hinterland, which he named Markland ("forest land"). Markland is the most readily identifiable of the countries mentioned in the sagas and has been widely accepted to be the Labrador coast south of Cape Porcupine, a remarkable feature of which is an extensive white sand beach.

Sailing two days from Markland, driven by a northeast wind, Leif's crew came to a third country and, according to the *Greenlanders' Saga*:

> *They went ashore and looked about them. The weather was fine. There was dew on the grass, and the first thing they did was to get some of it on their hands and put it to their lips, and to them it seemed the sweetest thing they had ever tasted. Then they went back to their ship and sailed into the sound that lay between the island and the headland jutting out to the north.*
>
> *They steered a westerly course round the headland. There were extensive shallows there and at low tide their ship was left high and dry, with the sea almost out of sight. But they were so impatient to land that they could not bear to wait for the rising tide to float the ship; they ran ashore to a place where a river flowed out of a lake ... they anchored the ship, carried their hammocks ashore and put up booths. Then they decided to winter there, and build some large houses.*
>
> *There was no lack of salmon in the river or the lake, bigger salmon than they had ever seen. The country seemed to them so kind that no winter fodder would be needed for livestock: there was never any frost all winter and grass hardly withered.* [1]

In the course of exploring this new country, Tyrkir, who is described as a "southerner" and was probably a German, excitedly proclaimed that he had found grapes. Leif gave the country the name Vinland ("wine land"). After wintering, the party made up a cargo of timber and filled the ship's boat with grapes and vines.

It was probably the forests described by Bjarni that made Leif so

---

1   Magnus Magnusson and Herman Palsson (trans.) *The Vinland Sagas: The Norse Discovery of America.* London: Penguin Books, 1965. p.54-58.

determined to explore the new country. For a seafaring people in barren Greenland, wood was a much-valued commodity and the accounts in the sagas of each of the Vinland voyages make it clear that cutting timber was the means to finance such voyages. The cutting of grapes and vines is also frequently mentioned. It was these "grapes" more than anything else that gave a mythological character to "Vinland the Good" and seem to have assured that some knowledge of the place persisted in Iceland long after the obscure end of the Greenland colony. It is the prominence given to grapes and wine that makes it difficult for many to identify Vinland with northern Newfoundland, despite indisputable evidence of Norse settlement at L'Anse aux Meadows. Those who accept that L'Anse aux Meadows was indeed the site of Vinland have suggested that the "wild grapes" were more likely berries and that Leif was following his father's practice of "giving a land a good name" to make it more attractive.

Throughout the nineteenth century, the theory that the Icelandic sagas did indeed describe an attempt to settle North America (nearly

W.A. Munn. (Courtesy the *Newfoundland Quarterly*.)

In the early 1900s, a Newfoundland businessman and amateur historian, William Munn, more fully developed the theory that Vinland could be found in northern Newfoundland. Munn suggested that L'Anse aux Meadows was a likely site of Leif's original landfall in Vinland. Munn proposed that the search for remains of the colony should begin in nearby Pistolet Bay.

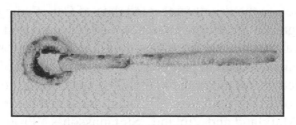

The Norse cloak-pin found at L'Anse aux
Meadows. (Courtesy Parks Canada.)

In the 1960s, Norwegian explorer Helge Ingstadt began a systematic
search in northern Newfoundland and, on landing at L'Anse aux
Meadows, was told by local resident George Decker that there were
indeed the ruins of something in a field near the community. Having
some experience with archaeological work then under way in
Greenland, Ingstadt recognized the low mounds in the field as the
remains of turf walls. The site was subsequently excavated by
Ingstadt's wife, archaeologist Anne Stine, and later by Parks Canada.
They found the remains of three large turf houses and five
outbuildings (including what was probably a blacksmith's forge) — as
well as 130 artifacts: nails, a soapstone spindle whorl, a stone lamp
and a bronze cloak-pin.

Anne Stine Ingstad at L'Anse aux Meadows. (Courtesy
Provincial Archives of Newfoundland and Labrador.)

500 years before the usually-accepted date of Cabot's voyage discovery) gained increasing credence. Several scholars tentatively identified Labrador or northern Newfoundland as the most likely sites for Vinland, based in part on the "Stefannsson map", which was compiled in Iceland in the late 1500s, but is presumed to have been based on earlier tradition. This map indicated the locations of Helluland, Markland and Vinland. Stefannsson's "Promontorium Winlandia" does indeed seem likely to be a representation of the Great Northern Peninsula of Newfoundland.

Although the site has been radiocarbon dated to approximately AD 1000, scholars have not universally accepted the contention that L'Anse aux Meadows is Vinland. Some have suggested that the site may not have been the main colony of the Norse, but rather a boat-repair station or other seasonal site, at the "entrance to Vinland". Still, L'Anse aux Meadows contains the only indisputable archaeological evidence of the Norse presence in North America and is hence one of the most important historic sites on the continent (see plate III).

Shortly (see plate III) after Leif's return from Vinland, his father Eirik died. So it is presumed that the explorer settled down in his role as head of the family at Eiriksfjord. Leif's brother, Thorvald, decided on a further voyage of exploration. Thorvald obtained permission to use Leif's ship and his *budir* ("booths" or, to adopt the Newfoundland term for a makeshift shelter, "tilts") in Vinland. Thorvald's party reached Leif's tilts and caught fish for their winter's food. The next spring, a small party explored the coast to the west in the ship's boat, where "they found the country very attractive, with woods stretching almost down to the shore and white sandy beaches." The following summer, Thorvald took the ship east, then north along the coast. There the Norse first encountered the Skraelings ("screechers" or "savages"), asleep under their skin boats on a sandy beach. The Norse killed eight of the nine Skraelings at this first encounter and soon had to withstand an attack, during which Thorvald was fatally wounded by an arrow in his armpit. After one more winter at "Leif's tilts" (*Leifsbudir*), the Norse returned to Greenland with their cargo.

On hearing of Thorvald's death, another of Eirik's sons, Thorstein, decided to fetch home his brother's body. But Thorstein's ship was driven back to Greenland, where he spent the winter at the Western Settlement and died of a sickness. The next summer Thorvald's widow, Gudrid, returned to Eiriksfjord, where she was courted by Thorfinn Karlsefni, the owner of a trading ship. Eventually, Leif agreed to let his sister-in-law remarry, while "there was the same talk about Vinland voyages as before, and everyone, including Gudrid, kept urging Karlsefni to make the voyage."

While both Leif and Thorvald had been scouting new lands to settle (and indeed Thorvald had decided where to build his home just before his death), the primary purpose of such voyages appears to have been to make up cargoes for Greenland. Karlsefni, however, took a larger party — numbering 60 men and five women, as well as "livestock of all kinds" — and seems to have intended to set up a colony. On arriving at Leif's tilts, the Norse soon had plenty of supplies, for "a fine big rorqual [whale] was driven ashore". From the *Saga*:

> *The first winter passed into summer, and then they had their first encounter with Skraelings, when a great number of them came out of the wood one day. The cattle were grazing near by and the bull began to bellow and roar with great vehemence. This terrified the Skraelings and they fled, carrying their packs, which contained furs and sables and pelts of all kinds. They made for Karlsefni's houses and tried to get inside, but Karlsefni had the doors barred against them. Neither side could understand the other's language.*
>
> *Then the Skraelings put down their packs and opened them up and offered their contents, preferably in exchange for weapons; but Karlsefni forbade his men to sell arms. Then he hit on the idea of telling the women to carry milk out to the Skraelings, and when the Skraelings saw the milk they wanted to buy nothing else. The outcome of their trading expedition was that the Skraelings carried their purchases away in their bellies, and left their packs and furs with Karlsefni and his men.*
>
> *After that, Karlsefni ordered a strong wooden palisade to be erected round the houses, and they settled in. About this time Karlsefni's wife, Gudrid, gave birth to a son, and he was named Snorri.*

Early next winter the Skraelings returned, in much greater numbers this time, bringing with them the same kind of wares as before. Karlsefni told the women, ''You must carry out to them the same produce that was most in demand last time, and nothing else.'' As soon as the Skraelings saw the milk, they threw their packs in over the palisade. ...

'Now we must devise a plan'', said Karlsefni, ''for I expect they will pay us a third visit, and this time with hostility and in greater numbers. This is what we must do: ten men are to go out on the headland here and make themselves conspicuous and the rest of us are to go into the wood and make a clearing there, where we can keep our cattle when the Skraelings come out of the forest. We shall take our bull and keep him to the fore.'' (The place where they intended to have their encounter with the Skraelings had the lake on one side and the woods on the other.)

Karlsefni's plan was put into effect, and the Skraelings came right to the place that Karlsefni had chosen for the battle. The fighting began, and many of the Skraelings were killed. There was one tall and handsome man among the Skraelings and Karlsefni reckoned that he must be their leader. One of the Skraelings had picked up an axe, and after examining it for a moment, he swung it at a man standing beside him, who fell dead at once. The tall man then took hold of the axe, looked at it for a moment, and then threw it as far as he could out into the water. Then the Skraelings fled into the forest as fast as they could, and that was the end of the encounter.

Karlsefni and his men spent the whole winter there, but in the spring he announced that he had no wish to stay there any longer and wanted to return to Greenland. They made ready for the voyage and took with them much valuable produce, vines and grapes and pelts. They put to sea and reached Eiriksfjord safely and spent the winter there. Now there was renewed talk of voyaging to Vinland, for these expeditions were considered a good source of fame and fortune. [2]

2   Magnus Magnusson and Herman Palsson (trans.) *The Vinland Sagas.*

In the popular literature, it is Leif Eiriksson whose name is, more than any other, associated with the Vinland voyages. Yet Leif spent only one winter at Vinland, while Thorvald Eiriksson and Thorfinn Karlsefni each spent three years in the newly-discovered land. It is also worthy to note the role that women played in the settling and exploration of Vinland. Both Gudrid and Freydis were major players in the Vinland sagas, in contrast to the peripheral role played by women in the subsequent exploration of Newfoundland. (There have been, incidentally, several historical novels written about the Norse in Vinland — including Eiriksdottir by Joan Clark, which is told from the point of view of Freydis.)

Interior of one of the reconstructed Norse dwellings. (Courtesy Parks Canada.)

The next expedition to Vinland, and the last recorded in the sagas, was conceived by Eirik's daughter, Freydis. During the summer that Karlsefni returned to Greenland, two Icelandic brothers, Helgi and Finnbogi, arrived from Norway with a cargo. They spent the winter at Eiriksfjord, where they were approached by Freydis to mount a joint expedition to Vinland. This expedition included two boats, each carrying 30 men and some women (there were five women in the Icelandic vessel and probably the same number travelling with Freydis) — although Freydis is said to have concealed an extra five men from her partners.

The brothers reached Leif's tilts first and began moving in. But Freydis objected and the brothers moved further inland on the bank of a lake. During the winter, an attempt to reconcile the two parties by holding "games and entertainments" degenerated into further bad feeling and "all visiting between the houses ceased". In the spring, Freydis visited Helgi and Finnbogi, suggesting a reconciliation and an exchange of vessels to allow her party to return to Greenland with a cargo. According to the *Greenlanders Saga*, Freydis then returned to her husband and claimed that she had been insulted and abused by Helgi and Finnbogi. She threatened her husband with divorce unless he avenged her honour and succeeded in goading him into killing the Icelanders and their men. Freydis herself is said to have put the women in the party to death, when the Greenlanders hesitated. Sworn to secrecy, the party returned to Greenland that summer, where the truth eventually came out.

The settling and exploration of Vinland was a brief, if dramatic, episode in the annals of the Greenland colony. It appears likely that at least some contact with Vinland was maintained in the subsequent history of Greenland. Other Icelandic records have fragmentary references to Vinland and Markland — including a voyage by the Bishop of Greenland in 1121 * and a brief mention of a Greenland ship storm-blown to Iceland with a cargo from Markland in 1347.

The Greenland colony became increasingly isolated, even from Iceland, after about AD 1200, when a general cooling of the earth's

---

* The Sagas do not mention whether he returned.

climate resulted in increased sea ice, barring the usual routes between Iceland and Greenland. Scholars now speculate that the Greenland colony eventually died out about the time that North America was rediscovered by Europeans. If only we had some written record of the stories of Vinland that must have been told among Eirik's descendants in Greenland!

For the most part, the above account of the Norse experience in Vinland is based upon the *Greenlanders Saga* — generally considered the more reliable of the two Icelandic sagas which relate the story of Vinland. Scholars have determined that *Eiriks Saga* is likely a later adaption of much of the same material.

There are, however, important differences between the two. According to *Eirik's Saga*, the new lands were first reached by Leif Eiriksson, while many of the later events and voyages would seem to have been combined into one voyage by Thorfinn Karlsefni. Freydis and Thorvald both participated in this expedition, which numbered 160 people, with Thorvald being killed by an arrow fired by a "Uniped" or one-legged being. This saga mentions two locations or settlements: *Straumfjord* and *Hop*. It also seems to suggest that the Karlsefni expedition eventually broke up into three parties: the settlement at Straumfjord, a "southern party" at Hop, and a splinter group to the north under one "Thorhall the Hunter", which eventually reached Ireland. This division would seem to result from a continuing search for Vinland, which in *Eirik's Saga* does not seem to have been found by Karlsefni. This saga does, however, also make reference to grapes and wild wheat — discovered by two Scots in this version.

Eirik's Saga also contains an intriguing reference to two Skraeling boys being taken captive, who "said that there was a country across from their own land where the people went about in white clothing and uttered loud cries and carried poles with patches of cloth attached." The saga goes on to suggest that this place might be *Hvitramannaland* ("White Men's Land" or Greater Ireland) which has been seized upon as supporting evidence by advocates of an Irish discovery of North America.

Both of the "Vinland sagas" end by listing the descendants of Thorfinn Karlsefni, who settled in Iceland after his adventures, and who is presumed to have been the major source for what has been recorded about Vinland. From the *Greenlander's Saga*:

> *A great many people are descended from Karlsefni; he has become the ancestor of a prolific line. It was Karlsefni himself who told more fully than anyone else the story of all these voyages, which has been to some extent recorded here.*

Given their source, it is not surprising that the sagas do not mention further visits by the Greenlanders to Helluland, Markland or Vinland. However, such visits do indeed seem quite possible, in that the Greenlanders remained perennially short of both metal and wood and that this situation would have worsened as the isolation from Europe continued. Since Markland would at least have offered bog iron and wood for both smelting the iron and ship-building, it seems likely that some contact continued beyond the 10–20 years covered by the Icelandic sagas.

Archaeology has also provided a few thin threads of evidence of more sustained contact. These include a Norse coin from about 1065–1080 unearthed in Maine (found in association with pieces of Ramah chert, which might suggest that these items may have been traded or seized and brought to the south) as well as metal fragments found in association with Inuit artifacts in Ungava Bay and elsewhere in Arctic Canada.

The Norse referred to all the native peoples they encountered as "Skraelings" — which means "screechers" or "savages". Some details in the Sagas suggest an Eskimo people (i.e. the use of skin boats), but the Straits of Belle Isle area at this time was peopled by ancestral Innu and/or Beothuk as well.

Although it appears that some trade may have taken place in later years, the hostile contacts with the Skraelings in Vinland were undoubtedly the major factor in beating back the Norse, the first time that they tried to settle a country that was already occupied. Unlike later European explorers, the Norse did not have the great advantage over the natives that was later to be provided by gunpowder. Further, the Greenland colony was seemingly too small and too isolated to carry the communicable diseases that were to prove devastating to the natives when the European next encountered the aboriginal inhabitants of North America.

3.

John Cabot, 1497 & 1498.

"Hym that found the new Isle".

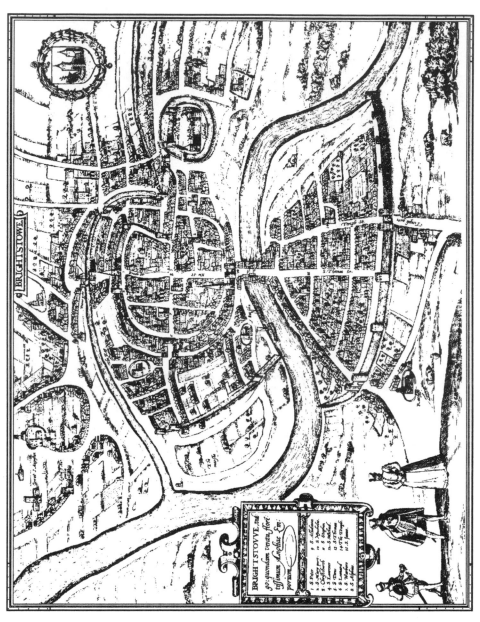

Bristol in 1572. In 1498 John Cabot had a house at St. Nicholas Street, approximately at the centre of this map. His voyage presumably embarked from "y Backe" nearby, or from "The Key" at top. (From the British Library.)

In December 1497, Raimondo di Soncino, an Italian merchant in London, wrote to the Duke of Milan concerning new lands which had recently been discovered to the west:

> ... *[it may not weary you to hear how] the King has gained a great part of Asia without a stroke of the sword. In this kingdom is a popular Venetian called Zoane Caboto, a man of considerable ability, most skilful in navigation, who having seen the most serene kings, first him of Portugal, then him of Spain, that they had occupied unknown islands, thought to make a similar acquisition for His Majesty [Henry VII of England]. And having obtained the royal privileges which gave him the use of the land found by him, provided the right of possession was reserved to the Crown, he departed in a little ship from Bristol with 18 persons, who placed their fortunes with him. Passing Ibernia [Ireland] more to the west, and then ascending towards the north, he began to navigate the eastern part of the ocean, leaving for some days the north to the right hand, and having wandered enough he came at last to firm land, where he planted the royal banners, took possession for his Highness, made certain marks, and returned.*
>
> *The said Messer Zoane, as he is a foreigner and poor, would not be believed if his partners, who are all Englishmen, and from Bristol, did not testify to the truth of what he tells. This Messer Zoane has the description of the world in a chart, and also in a solid globe which he has made, and he shows where he landed. ... The sea is full of fish which are taken not only with the net but also with a basket in which a stone is put so that the basket sinks into the water...*
>
> *And the Englishmen, his partners, say that they can bring so many fish that the kingdom will have no more need of Islanda [Iceland], and that from this country there will be a very great trade in the fish they call stock fish.* [3]

3   · Prowse, D.W. *A History of Newfoundland.* Belleville, Ont.: Mika Studio, 1972. p.11.

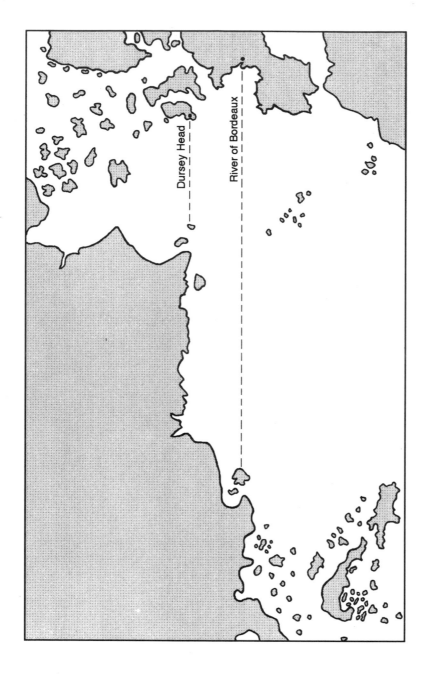

A representation of the La Cosa map of North America from 1500. Lines of latitude, extended from Dursey Head in Ireland and the "River of Bordeaux" in France, correspond with La Cosa's "sea discovered by the English" and are the first cartographic representation of the New-Founde-Land. (Map by Kathy Hudson).

Labels within the map: Dursey Head, River of Bordeaux

Soncino's letter is one of several communications from various merchants and ambassadors in England to their masters in Italy and Spain and which, between them, provide most of what is known about John Cabot's voyage of discovery in the summer of 1497. The Soncino letter provides historians with some useful facts concerning the voyage, but little which can positively identify the new lands discovered. Cabot's map and globe have long since been lost. Historians have not been able to unearth any first-hand account of the voyage from a participant. It may be that there are other documents, mouldering in some European archive, which may yet shed further light on John Cabot's discoveries. After all, the single most important document concerning Cabot's voyage, the "John Day letter", was not discovered until 1955 — by an American scholar working in the Archivo de Simancas in Spain. But for the moment, those attempting to reconstruct Cabot's pioneering voyage, are left with a task that is, in the words of historian S. E. Morison, "like trying to construct a big picture puzzle from one per cent of the pieces".

While what we do not know about John Cabot could fill volumes what is known about the explorer's life before 1497 can be easily summarized. He was born in Genoa, Italy, in the mid-fifteenth century — the son of a merchant, Giulio Caboto. In his youth, his family moved to Venice (Cabot lived there for 15 years before 1476). At that time, Venice was the pre-eminent centre of maritime trade for southern Europe—its prosperity and influence having grown with the spice trade between Europe and the Arab lands of the Near East. Soncino notes that Cabot had been to Mecca, so he was presumably engaged in this trade. That trade was the origin of Cabot's plan to reach the source of these valuable goods, by sailing west — specifically to reach the island of Cipangu (Japan). Cipangu was suggested by the Venetian traveller Marco Polo, as the source of the spices, gold, and jewels of the Orient.

Cabot had married a woman named Mattea and by 1484 had a family of sons living in Venice. On the evidence of the Soncino letter, it would appear Cabot had taken his scheme for a voyage of discovery before the courts of Portugal and Spain. Perhaps Cabot was promoting his voyage, at the same time that another native of Genoa, Christopher Columbus, was proposing a similar voyage. It seems logical that Cabot's efforts to obtain backing took place after Columbus' discovery of certain islands in the Caribbean in 1492. In the early 1490s, there are records of a Venetian, "John Cabot Montecalunya", resident in Valencia, Spain, where he prepared plans for harbour improvements. If this person was indeed the explorer John Cabot (and this is considered likely by most historians), then Cabot could have been in Valencia in April 1493, when Columbus passed through there on his way to Barcelona, to report the results of his own historic voyage.

By late 1495, Cabot had moved with his family to England. In 1496 he attempted a voyage of discovery out of the English port of Bristol, having obtained a grant of letters patent from the King, Henry VII, in March 1496. This voyage was aborted because of bad weather, disagreements among the crew, and shortage of food.

A second attempt was made in May 1497, in a navicula (or small ship) of about 50 tons, probably named the *Matthew* — or perhaps the *Mattea*, after Cabot's wife. The ship's company numbered either 18 or 20, and included Cabot, a Burgundian, a Genoese barber, at least two Bristol merchants, and a crew of Bristol seamen. Sailing past southern Ireland, to the west, Cabot sighted land after 35 days. Some sources have it that the landfall was on 24 June (at five o'clock in the morning, according to a map prepared by Cabot's son in 1544), which, reckoning backward, would give the date of departure from Bristol as 20 May. Cabot landed only at one place, in wooded country near his first sighting. He saw no people, but did note certain signs that convinced him that the country was inhabited. After sailing about for a month in coastal waters of the New-Founde-Land, he made his departure from a "cape of the mainland", (i.e. not a smaller island), which was said to be 1800 miles west of Dursey Head in Ireland.

The return voyage lasted only 15 days, bringing Cabot to the Brittany coast in early August. From there he returned to Bristol on 6 August, reporting to Henry VII a few days later, after which the King's daybooks record a payment of ten pounds "to hym that founde the new Isle".

Exactly where Cabot made land on 24 June 1497 has been much debated by historians over the past 500 years. The letter of John Day

The approach to Cape Bonavista, from an old chart.
(Courtesy Provincial Archives of Newfoundland.)

(written in late 1497 or early 1498) is the only surviving document that provides details about the course of the voyage. Day was an English merchant with business contacts in Spain. He addresses his letter to "El Almirante Mayor"(loosely translated as "Grand Admiral"). Christopher Columbus was one of only two men in Spain entitled to be addressed by this title and most historians feel justified in assuming that Columbus was the person addressed. The letter does not mention Cabot by name.

The Day letter appears to indicate that the coast traversed by Cabot stretched from the latitude of Dursey Head (about 51°33'N — i.e. approximately that of Cape Bauld, at the northern tip of Newfoundland) to latitude 45°35'N which is about the latitude of the south of the island of Newfoundland. Those who argue for a voyage entirely along the Newfoundland coast, point out that at latitude 45°40'N, Cape Race is only about 100 kilometres north of the latitude of the mouth of the Garrone (the "River Bordeaux" of the Day letter).

Although the John Day letter is certainly the single most important evidence regarding the John Cabot voyage of 1497, historians are not entirely agreed as to how it is to be interpreted. To begin with, a map or chart that accompanied the original letter was not found — and key passages of the letter refer the reader to this map. Day wrote in Spanish which was not his native tongue and the scholars have small, but crucial differences of opinion as to how certain sections should be accurately translated. There is also some question as to how much faith should be put in the latitudes indicated by the letter: By the methods of navigation in use at the time, errors of one degree or more in reckoning latitude were common. If Cabot landed only at one point, at least one of the measurements taken must have been made at sea — increasing the chance of an error.

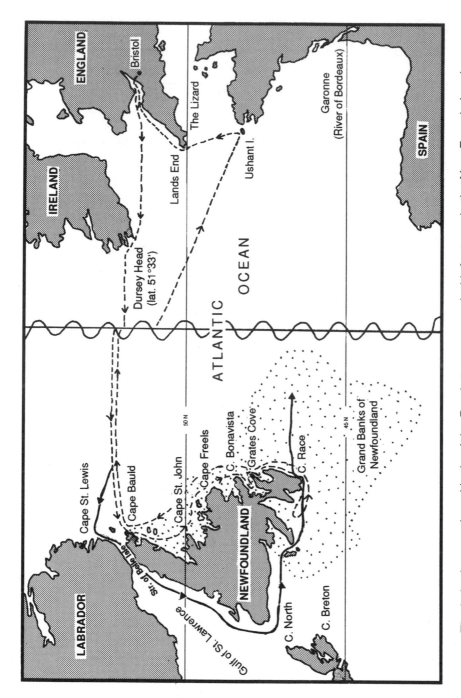

The latitudes mentioned in the John Day letter compared with features in the New-Founde-Land, with representations of two of the many conjectured routes for Cabot's voyage of 1497.

Before looking further at the questions raised by John Day's letter to Columbus, it might be well to read the text as it was translated:

...I am sending a copy of the land which has been found ... From the said copy your Lordship will learn what you wish to know, for in it are named the capes of the mainland and the islands, and thus you will see where land was first sighted, since most of the land was discovered after turning back.

Thus your Lordship will know that the cape referred to nearest to Ireland is 1800 miles west of Dursey Head which is in Ireland, and the southernmost part of the Island of the Seven Cities is west of Bordeaux River, and your Lordship will know that he landed at only one spot of the mainland, near the place where land was first sighted, and they disembarked there with a crucifix and raised banners with the arms of the Holy Father and those of the King of England, my master; and they found tall trees of the kind masts are made, and other smaller trees, and the country is very rich in grass. In that particular spot, as I told your Lordship, they found a trail that went inland, they saw a site where a fire had been made, they saw manure of animals which they thought to be farm animals, and they saw a stick half a yard long pierced at both ends, carved and painted with brazil, and by such sights they believe the land to be inhabited. Since he was with just a few people, he did not dare advance inland beyond the shooting distance of the cross-bow, and after taking in fresh water he returned to his ship. All along the coast they found many fish like those which in Iceland are dried in the open and sold in England and other countries, and these fish are called in English 'stockfish'; and thus following the shore they saw two forms running on land one after the other, but they could not tell if they were human beings or animals; and it seemed to them that there were fields where they thought might also be villages, and they saw a forest whose foliage looked beautiful.

They left England toward the end of May, and must have been on the way 35 days before sighting land; the wind was east - north-east and the sea calm going and coming back, except for one day when he ran into a storm two or three days before

*finding land; and going so far out, his compass needle failed to
point north and marked two rhumbs below. They spent about
one month discovering the coast and from the above mentioned
cape of the mainland which is nearest to Ireland, they returned
to the coast of Europe in fifteen days. They had the wind behind
them, and he reached Brittany because the sailors confused
him, saying that he was heading too far north. From there he
came to Bristol, and he went to see the King to report to him all
the above mentioned; and the King granted him an annual
pension of twenty pounds sterling to sustain himself until the
time comes when more will be known of this business, since
with God's help it is hoped to push through plans for exploring
the said land more thoroughly next year with ten or twelve
vessels — because in his voyage he had only one ship of fifty
'toneles' and twenty men and food for seven or eight months —
and they want to carry out this new project.*

*It is considered certain that the cape of the said land was
found and discovered in the past by the men from Bristol who
found 'Brasil' as your Lordship well knows. It was called the
Island of Brasil, and it is assumed and believed to be the
mainland that the men from Bristol found.* [4]

This last paragraph raises another point that has become an
historical controversy: whether Cabot was indeed making for a land
that was already known to certain merchants of Bristol. At that time,
Bristol was one of England's largest ports, second only to London.
Indeed, Bristol surpassed London in its trading connections in the
neighbouring Atlantic, particularly in the trade in wines with Spain
and Portugal and in the import of fish from Iceland. After 1478, the
Icelandic fishery was being deliberately closed to English fishermen
and traders by a new governor, Diddrik Pining.

British historian David Beers Quinn has shown that from about
1480 there is a well-established belief that a number of ships left

---

4   Cumming, W.P; Skelton, R.A.; Quinn, D.B. *The Discovery of North
     America*. Toronto: McClelland and Stewart, 1971. p.80

Bristol searching for the legendary "Isle of Brasil". That these voyages continued over a period of years, may well be regarded as evidence that something of commercial significance (such as a new fishing ground) might have been found. There are also indications in some documents that Bristol merchants Hugh Elyot and Robert Thorne discovered a new island in the West in about 1494. Certainly, these two were among the first Europeans whose attempts to exploit the fisheries in the New-Founde-Land are documented, in 1501. It seems that their early interest in the New-Founde-Land stems from being involved in John Cabot's voyages.

After having made the first voyage with no royal financial support (other than letters patent) — "on his own proper charges", as well as the presumed backing of merchants of Bristol, John Cabot was now making a considerable impression in London. As a Venetian merchant in London, Lorenzo Pasqualigo, wrote to his brothers:

> *The king has promised him for the spring ten armed ships. ... he is called the Great Admiral and vast honour is paid to him and he goes dressed in silk, and these English run after him like mad, and indeed he can enlist as many of them as he pleases, and a number of rogues as well.* [5]

For John Cabot's second voyage, with the authorization and encouragement of Henry VII, five ships and 300 men proposed to make the voyage, early in 1498. The King either provided or equipped one vessel, with the remaining four being provided by Bristol interests, and supplied by merchants from that port and from London. The ships were provisioned for one year and carried cargoes of trade goods, intending to establish a "colony" in the New-Founde-Land, from whence trade might be carried on with Cathay and Cipangu (which Cabot continued to assume were nearby). The ships sailed from Bristol in early May. One vessel, damaged by a storm, put in at Ireland and did not continue the voyage. Some of those involved in the voyage are known to have

---

5   Williamson, J.A. *The Cabot Voyages and Bristol: Discovery under Henry VII.* Cambridge: Cambridge University Press, 1962. p.208.

survived. It is possible to interpret the documents to suggest that at least one vessel returned from the voyage. But, it might well be that these survivors were only the ones aboard the vessel that turned back from Ireland.

We have no way of knowing for certain whether the second Cabot voyage ever reached New-Founde-Land waters. Or, if this were the case, that any report of the voyage ever reached Europe. However, in the summer of 1501, Portuguese crewmen from one of Gaspar Corte Real's vessels obtained from natives, probably on the Newfoundland coast, a piece of a sword of Italian workmanship and two Venetian earrings. It has been concluded that the second Cabot voyage was the most likely source of these items, because Cabot's first voyage did not encounter any natives and landed only in one place.

The last word in the narrative of the second Cabot voyage belongs to the English court historian, Polydore Vergil:

> *In the event he is believed to have found the new lands nowhere but on the very bottom of the ocean, to which he is thought to have descended together with his boat, the victim himself of that self-same ocean; since after that voyage he was never seen again anywhere.*

If there is any cartographic evidence of either of the Cabot voyages (as with so many aspects of the Cabot mystery, historians are again divided), then the best place to look is to what is known as the "La Cosa map". This map of the world is presumed to be a copy of a map prepared about 1500 by the Spanish navigator Juan de la Cosa. It shows some representation of the islands of the Caribbean, flanked to the north and south by sketchy outlines of the coasts of North and South America (see plate IV). La Cosa, who accompanied the second Columbus voyage to the new world, had some personal knowledge of the Caribbean area. The most intriguing part of this map is a section of the North American coast marked by five English flags. It names 22 features on this coast, the easternmost cape being *Cavo de ynglaterra* (Cape of England), with a gulf to the west of the "named coast" designated *mar descubierto por inglese* (sea discovered by the English). It is thought that this representation of an English coast must reflect Cabot's voyage of 1497 — or, just maybe, although this is considered less likely, the voyage of 1498. For the most part, the questions as to where exactly Cabot landed have depended upon interpretations of the La Cosa map and the John Day letter.

With the Cabot anniversary occurring in 1997, the question as to where exactly Cabot first sighted land will be raised more than once, along with the question as to where he landed (for the first sight of land was near the actual landing). In the past, historians have suggested landfalls at a wide range of possible sites — virtually the whole eastern seaboard of North America, from Labrador to Massachusetts; however, the unearthing of the John Day letter at least had the effect of narrowing the search. Let us examine some of the suggested landfalls:

CAPE BONAVISTA

In 1895, the great Newfoundland historian Daniel Woodley Prowse pronounced that Cape Bonavista was Cabot's landfall, based on three grounds: that Bonavista, in Italian, is "O good sight"; that an "unbroken tradition points to Cape Bonavista" as the land first seen; and that a map made by John Mason in about 1625 contains the legend *A Caboto primum reperta* (first found by Cabot) opposite the Cape. Judge Prowse sums up magisterially: "On this ground, and for other reasons, as a Newfoundlander, I claim for Bonavista the honour of being the first land seen in North America." He goes on to identify nearby King's Cove as the harbour where the explorer landed and raised the King's arms. Prowse's pronouncement has been the key in firmly establishing as a "true fact" in the minds of many Newfoundlanders that Cabot landed at Cape Bonavista.

Prowse reached his conclusions without having the benefit of one of the essential pieces of evidence available to modern scholars — namely the John Day letter. Indeed, on the first reading, the Day letter would seem to provide grounds for dismissing Prowse's claim. Yet, while it is possible to infer the northern and southern limits of the coasts explored from the evidence of the Day letter, nowhere does the letter identify the point at which land was first sighted, with either "the cape nearest Ireland" or "the southernmost part of the

Island". Rather, on the question of the landfall, Day merely refers the reader to the long-lost accompanying map — "thus you will see where land was first sighted".

There is nothing in the Day letter that contradicts the theory of a voyage making land at Cape Bonavista, then a sailing to the south before doubling back toward Cape Bauld and departure. Of course, this argument applies just as well to a landfall at Grates Point, or Cape Freels, or Cape St. John. Former Newfoundland Lieutenant Governor Fabian O'Dea (a lawyer, noted map-collector, and a student of early Newfoundland cartography) has concluded that a good case can be made for Cape Bonavista "as the most likely landfall" — basing his conclusion, in part, on arguments raised by Morison to support the thesis that the landfall was actually at Cape DeGrat, near the northernmost tip of the New-Founde-Land.

CAPE DeGRAT (The tip of the New-Founde-Land)

In terms of his unequivocal certainty about the correctness of his own conclusions, Judge Prowse can only be matched by the great American historian of the age of discovery, Samuel Eliot Morison. Morison's conclusion that the actual landfall was Cape DeGrat probably has the widest acceptance.

With a sound practical knowledge of sailing and the sea, Morison, more than any other historian, made a concerted effort to identify coastal features from the available accounts of the age of exploration. His hypothesis is as follows:

Cabot would have made his departure from Dursey Head, perhaps because of reports current in Bristol that the "Isle of Brasil" was to be found in this latitude, and because late-medieval voyagers normally took their departure from points of known latitude. The explorer would then have sailed more or less due west — a practice known as latitude sailing. This was in keeping with methods used in the open ocean by European navigators of the time — by periodically measuring the elevation of the north star or the noonday sun and endeavouring to steer a course that kept the latitude constant. Cabot then made land at what we now call Cape DeGrat, just to the south of the northernmost tip of Newfoundland at Cape Bauld. Cape DeGrat had a high elevation and would be the point of land first seen by a vessel approaching from the east. Morison proposes Griquet harbour as the point where Cabot landed, with a coasting voyage south and east to Cape Race, then west as far as Cape St. Mary's. In crossing Placentia Bay, Cabot would have been unable to sound bottom with a 100-fathom lead line and, being unable to see the low-lying land of the Burin Peninsula to the west, turned back.

In his *Canada rediscovered* (1991), Robert McGhee, head of the scientific section of the Archaeological Survey of Canada at the Canadian Museum of Civilization, concludes that "Morison's interpretation... does seem to be the one that best fits the information contained in John Day's letter". In *John Cabot: the discovery of Newfoundland* (1994), Newfoundland writer and cartographic technician B. D. Fardy lends his unqualified support to Morison's reasoning.

Morison answers those who would point out that the John Day letter clearly states that the majority of the land was discovered on the return voyage by pointing out that the word "discovered" could as easily be translated as "explored". At the time, even in English, the two words were used almost interchangeably. By this reasoning, the portion of the voyage returning to Cape DeGrat would naturally be the time to investigate the new lands more fully. Also, it would be a little odd for Cabot to have embarked on his return journey (after a coasting voyage of about one month) without stopping to replenish his supply of fresh water. If a voyage doubling back to the original landfall is allowed, then Cabot might have stopped again at his original landing place for water. The Day letter says that "he landed at only one spot of the mainland" rather than that he landed only one time. But, this is splitting hairs.

GRATES POINT/ COVE

In 1873, W. E. Cormack, a pioneer explorer of the Newfoundland interior proposed Grates Point as the Cabot landfall — although, in keeping with the mistaken conventional wisdom of the time, he ascribed the discovery to Sebastian Cabot. (The primacy of the father was not restored until the 1880s.) Cormack states that "[Cabot] recorded the event by cutting an inscription, still perfectly legible, on a large block of rock that stands on the shore." In the early 1900s, Newfoundland businessman and historian W. A. Munn

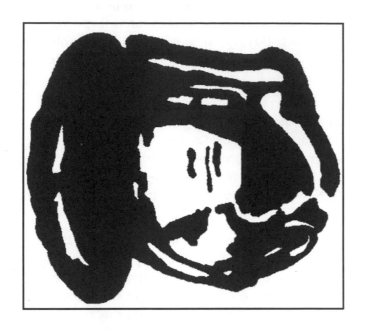

Judge D.W. Prowse wrote in 1895 "Alas! for the glory of our Island... there are no portraits to discuss." In 1881 the designers of this Venetian medallion imagined Caboto a bearded, Renaissance cosmographer. (Courtesy Parks Canada.) In 1997 it was decided that Cabot's official image would be that of a youthful, square-jawed hero. (Courtesy Cabot 500.)

52

examined the "Grates Cove Stone" and found several inscriptions, badly weathered, none of which seemed to have any relevance to Cabot. Later, the curator of the Newfoundland Museum, L. E. F. English, claimed that he was able to decipher an inscription "IO CAB". Finally, there is vague speculation that on his second voyage, Cabot was wrecked on Baccalieu Island, just off Grates Point.

LABRADOR

Before the publication of the Day letter, a Labrador landfall, near Cape St. Lewis, was favoured by many scholars, and was revived by Melvin Jackson of the Smithsonian Institute in the early 1960s. Several sixteenth and seventeenth century maps have a note on English discovery in this area. Those favouring Labrador could also point to Sebastian Cabot's description of the new land as containing white bears. However, Jacques Cartier's account of meeting a polar bear off the northeast coast of Newfoundland in 1534, provides grounds for suggesting that polar bears were once more common on the Island. At latitude 52°20'N, Cape St. Lewis or Cape Charles could be the "cape nearest Ireland" of the Day letter, given some error. However, in June month, the amount of ice normally encountered on the Labrador coast has led many to conclude that a more southerly landfall is likely.

Jackson's conclusion favours a Labrador landfall, followed by a voyage through the Strait of Belle Isle and along the western and southern coasts of the New-Founde-Land, sailing south and west because Cabot believed it was in this direction that Cipangu was to be found. In his *John Cabot and Newfoundland*, commissioned for 1997 by the Newfoundland Historical Society, Alan F. Williams guardedly incorporates Jackson's theory into a "most likely" voyage.

OTHER LANDFALLS IN CONTENTION:

CAPE BRETON

This is the landfall favoured by historian D. B. Quinn, a notable English authority on the age of exploration and discovery. In careful academic fashion, Quinn states merely that Cape Breton "seems the least unlikely landfall''. The key elements contributing to his conclusion are that the Day letter would seem to indicate a voyage from west to east, for ''most of the land was discovered after turning back'' and the departure was made from ''the cape nearest Ireland''. As supporting evidence, some have suggested that the La Cosa map's legend ''sea discovered by the English'' appears next to a flag marking the landfall, at the western extremity of the named coast. By this interpretation, the marked ''sea'' is Cabot Strait, which was assumed to be a bay by many early explorers. Then too, there is a map prepared in 1544 with the assistance of John Cabot's son, Sebastian, which clearly identifies Cape Breton as the *prima terra vista* (land first seen). Those who support the argument for a Cape Breton landfall, believe that the majority of the Cabot voyage took place in New-Founde-Land waters, with the tips of the Burin and Avalon Peninsula's being the ''two islands'' seen on the larboard side, on the way back. In this interpretation, ''the cape nearest Ireland,'' would be the departure point, in the vicinity of Cape Race, south of St. John's.

MAINE

Not surprisingly, the theory of a Maine landfall, mostly exists in the United States. Its key elements are twofold:

First, that the La Cosa map shows a northern coastline that generally goes from west to east. The ''sea discovered by the English'' bears some resemblance to the Gulf of Maine. The coastline to the east resembles that of Maine and Nova Scotia. Their theory has a presumed landfall in what is now the southern part of that state and a point of departure in the vicinity of Cape Breton.

Second, that Cabot would have, unknowingly, drifted well to the south in the Labrador Current, bypassing Newfoundland in fog or rough weather. By this argument, the apparent indications of the latitudes of the lands discovered in the John Day letter result from errors in calculation and failure to make sufficient allowance for (magnetic declination) the variation between magnetic north and true north. Yet the Day letter does seem to indicate that Cabot was aware of declination: ''going so far out, his compass needle failed to point north and marked two rhumbs below''.

Before putting aside the controversy over Cabot's landfall, it might be well to sift once more, the evidence in contemporary records:

From the Pasqualigo letter (23 August 1497):

> ... he has discovered terra firma 700 leagues away... he coasted it for 300 leagues and landed and did not see any person...on the way back he saw two islands ... the tides are slack and do not run as they do here. [6]

From an anonymous and perhaps fanciful newsletter to the Duke of Milan (24 August 1497):

> ...he had returned safe, and has found two very large new islands. He has also discovered the Seven Cities, 400 leagues from England, on the western passage. [7]

From the Soncino letter (18 December 1497):

> ...the land is excellent and temperate, and they believe that Brazil wood and silk are native there. They assert that the sea is swarming with fish. [8]

From the Day letter (late December 1497 or January 1498):

> ...the cape nearest to Ireland is 1800 miles west of Dursey Head which is in Ireland, and the southernmost part of the Island of the Seven Cities is west of Bordeaux River... and they found tall trees of the kind masts are made, and other smaller trees, and the country is very rich in grass. ... All along the coast they found many fish like those which in Iceland are dried in the open and sold in England and other countries. ... [9]

6   Williamson, J.A. *The Cabot Voyages and Bristol: Discovery under Henry VII*. Cambridge: Cambridge University Press, 1962. p.208.

7   Williamson, J.A. *The Cabot Voyages and Bristol: Discovery under Henry VII*. Cambridge: Cambridge University Press, 1962. p.209.

8   Williamson, J.A. *The Cabot Voyages and Bristol: Discovery under Henry VII*. Cambridge: Cambridge University Press, 1962. p.210.

9   Cumming, W.P., Skelton, R.A. and Quinn, D.B. *The Discovery of North America*. Toronto: McClelland and Stewart, 1971. p. 80.

And finally, from the "Sebastian Cabot" map of 1544:

> ...*to a large island which is near the said land they gave the name Saint John, because it had been discovered the same day. ...There are ... many white bears, and very large stags like horses.* [10]

However, Sebastian Cabot also notes that the new land is inhabited by people "dressed in the skins of animals". Because Pasqualigo and Day both mention that no inhabitants were contacted on the first voyage, historians have concluded that Sebastian's description is based on a more northerly voyage — possible John Cabot's second, or the voyage which Sebastian Cabot made in about 1508.

It is not really appropriate to refer to John Cabot as having "discovered" Newfoundland, Canada, or North America. Obviously, there were many people living on this continent for centuries before 1497, and to speak of "discovery" therefore is incorrect. Newfoundland had already been "discovered" by Europeans at least once before, by the Norse.

Yet in 1497 there was little, if any, knowledge in Europe of the earlier Norse voyages to the New-Founde-Land. So Cabot's voyage was clearly a most significant event in history. It provided a certainty that there was a New-Founde-Land across the sea, and that the waters off this new land provided the prospect for a greater fishery than any previously known in the world.

This new knowledge did not offer the sought-after, shorter route to the riches of Asia. That quest was to continue, to no avail, for several hundred more years. Cabot's voyage, and the confirmation of great future prospects to the west, opened up the hundred-year Age of Discovery, and the exploration, and eventual European settlement, of North America.

---

10   Williamson, J.A. *The Cabot Voyages and Bristol: Discovery under Henry VII*. Cambridge: Cambridge University Press, 1962. p.207.

4.

Gaspar Corte Real, 1500 & 1501.
Miguel Corte Real, 1502.
João Fernandes, 1500 &1501.

"They have found land between the north and the west".

The Lisbon waterfront in the 16th century. (Bibliotheque Nationale, Paris.)

At the beginning of the 1400s, mariners of Genoa and Venice were the widest-ranging European navigators. From the beginning of the Crusades, these Italian city-states had been the most receptive to new ideas and products from the East. They soon became the main sea ports for the trade in spices, silks and other exotic goods from the Orient. The rise of empire of the Mongol Great Khan in northern Eurasia, had enabled competing caravan routes to be opened for this trade and a few Italian traders (the best known being the Venetian Marco Polo) had made the journey overland to "Cathay" (China). Following the collapse of the Mongol empire, the valuable commodities of the East were routed by water through the eastern Mediterranean, with the European-end of the trade again being dominated by Italians. Adapting Arab vessel design, and such advances in navigation as the magnetic compass, the Italians began to extend their sea-trade via routes through the Strait of Gibraltar to northern Europe — most particularly to the port cities of Flanders (modern-day Belgium), and also to London.

This trade had, as an important way-station, the Portuguese port of Lisbon. From about 1420, at the instigation of Prince Henry, the brother to the King of Portugal, Portugal began to take a very keen interest in maritime trade. Ultimately, Prince Henry "the Navigator", as he is known to history, encouraged studies in navigation, ship-building, and astronomy — in an all-encompassing attempt to extend the boundaries of the known world. At first, new Portuguese exploration was directed at North Africa. But as Prince Henry's collection of charts was supplemented by the work of Italian cartographers, the Prince began to take an interest in the many islands that these charts showed in the Ocean Sea (which we now know as western reaches of the Atlantic Ocean).

There were legends dating back to ancient Greece, that "Paradise" was to be found on an island or islands in mid-ocean. These were given the name *Insulae Fortunatae* (Happy Isles), or the Islands of the Blessed. Both these names were also associated with the Irish seafaring monk St. Brendan, because a popular account of his seventh-century travels described numerous islands discovered during an ocean voyage in quest of Paradise.

The demand for maps showing the Atlantic coastline of Europe

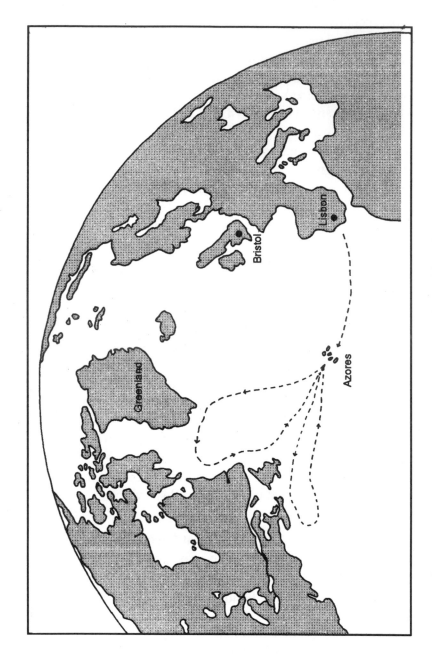

Conjectured routes of the Portuguese explorers, 1499-1503. (Map by Kathy Hudson).

grew along with trade. The custom became established of showing these mythical islands far out in the western ocean. Aside from St. Brendan's islands, two other mythical islands might be mentioned as having particular significance. Brasil, which by popular belief either floated or appeared every seven years, was frequently depicted off the coast of Ireland. Farther to the south was Antillia (or the Isle of the Seven Cities). According to Portuguese legend, the Seven Cities were populated by Christians who had been forced by the Moors to leave Portugal in the eighth century.

For the most part, the Portuguese search for geographical knowledge led in other directions than westward, into the boundless Ocean Sea. It was a subject of much curiosity as to which of these lands were the source of the spices of the East. One answer was suggested in the writings of Marco Polo, who had made a journey to Cathay and the court of the Great Khan in 1275. There he had heard of a rich island, still further to the east, which he identified as Cipangu (modern-day Japan). Polo's *Travels*, first published in about 1300, described Cipangu as situated in the "Sea of Chin" which contained:

> *''no fewer than seven thousand four hundred and forty four islands, mostly inhabited. … They produce many spices and drugs, particularly lignum-aloes and pepper, in great abundance, both white and black. It is impossible to estimate the value of the gold and other articles found in the islands.''* [11]

Because the earth was then known to be spherical (although estimates as to its size varied widely), some considered that it would be possible to reach Cipangu, and other rich islands in the east of the East, by sailing to the West, across the Ocean Sea. This was the dream that inspired the pioneering voyages of Christopher Columbus and John Cabot. Columbus hoped that Antillia, once discovered, would provide a staging point for trade with Cathay. Cabot entertained similar hopes for the fabled Isle of Brasil, as a

---

11   Davis, Kenneth C. *Don't Know Much About Geography.* New York: Avon Books, 1992. p.57.

way-station in opening trade with Cipangu. According to Raimondo di Soncino, while on a visit to Mecca and Cabot had asked those who

> *brought them, what was the place of origin of these spices, they answered they did not know, but that other caravans came with this merchandise to their homes from distant countries, and these again said that the goods had been brought to them from other remote regions. He therefore reasons that… always assuming that the earth is round, it follows as a matter of course that the last of all must take them in the north towards the west.* [12]

Prince Henry the Navigator had particular hopes that a sea route would be found around the continent of Africa, putting Portugal in the profitable middleman position in this important commerce. Portugal hoped to replace the Mediterranean traders. Accordingly, the primary focus of the Portuguese, in expanding knowledge in maritime matters, was to find a way to the south of Cape Bojador on the northwest African coast (south of present-day Morocco). Cape Bojador had long been considered by Europeans to be the southerly limit of navigation. It was believed, that the trade winds and ocean currents would prevent a ship that rounded the Cape from being able to return to Europe.

The perceived obstacle of rounding the African Cape Bojador was conquered by navigator Gil Eanes in 1434. But by this time, these voyages of exploration to the south had already led to the discovery of islands off Africa. The Madeiras had been rediscovered by about 1420, then colonized by Prince Henry. (One pioneer colonist was Bartholomew Perestrelo, whose daughter later married a young merchant-mariner named Christopher Columbus.)

In about 1431, Prince Henry had dispatched Gonzalo Velho west in search of the islands reported by St. Brendan. Far out in the ocean, Velho encountered shoals and islets, now known as the

---

12   Williamson, J.A. *The Cabot Voyages and Bristol: Discovery under Henry VII*. Cambridge: Cambridge University Press, 1962. p.210.

The Portuguese made crucial advances that would be later applied to the problems of high seas navigation. One important advance was the development of the caravel, a small ship, equipped with lateen sails on the Arab model. Caravels were much better able to sail into the wind than the square-sailed, unwieldy "cogs" normally used for most ocean trade. One Portuguese caravel carried out to sea by a storm, also made another crucial discovery — that if one sailed far out into the ocean from the African coast, contenting oneself with gradually gaining latitude, it was possible to reach a different zone of variable winds, that would support the return to Portugal. Once the ship had sailed far enough to the north, so that the north star or the noonday sun was at a similar altitude to that observed in Lisbon, the navigator could return home by simply sailing as near to due-east as possible.

Caravel. (From a map cartouche.)

Formigas. The next year, he discovered the most easterly of the Azores, the island named Santa Maria. In later years, vessels returning to Portugal from farther and farther south on the African coast, discovered other islands in this group, which lies in the approximate latitude of Lisbon. The most westerly islands of the Azores, Flores and Corvo, were not discovered until 1452. In 1456, the Cape Verde islands were discovered off the coast of Senegal. By Prince Henry's death in 1460, the Portuguese had established a profitable trade in gold and slaves with the Guinea coast and had colonized a number of islands, including the Azores.

In an attempt to gain new territories, the Kings of Portugal were well prepared to make finding an island worthwhile for the explorer. On many occasions, in the later part of the fifteenth century, the monarch issued charters to navigators going in search of new islands. These letters patent virtually gave the seaman and his heirs the discovered lands as a princedom — provided always that title remained with the King and that the proposed explorer found the new lands at his own expense. Alternatively, a new island might be granted to a royal favourite, who had the option of either ruling the lands in person, or sending out a "captain" to govern in his name.

In 1474, João Vaz Corte Real became Captain of the district known as Angra, on the Azorean island of Terceira (which took its name from having been the third of the archipelago discovered). Many Portuguese consider João Vaz Corte Real, the father of Gaspar and Miguel Corte Real, to have been the "real discoverer of America". This was based on a voyage he is supposed to have made to Greenland in 1472. However, scholars have dismissed this claim, noting that the voyage of João Vaz Corte Real and one Alvaro Martins Homem, is first mentioned more than 100 years after the supposed event, by a chronicler writing a history of the Azores. There is also the consideration that while the King of Portugal issued charters to many explorers for islands that they proposed to discover, no documents relating to this supposed voyage have come to light.

However, the last quarter of the 1400s did see numerous charters issued for such voyages to various Portuguese of the Azores. There are scant grounds for believing that any of these voyages reached North America, given prevailing winds and currents (even though Corvo is only 1000 miles from Cape Race). Yet there persisted the conviction that there were other islands to be discovered and ruled over, perhaps Antillia or Brasil, which many maps showed just beyond the Azores.

There were also rumours, and other signs, that there must be lands to the west. Had not Diogo de Teire, after his discovery of Corvo and Flores, sailed north and west to the latitude of Ireland and "found the winds to blow very brisk and the winds westerly and the sea to be very smooth, which they believed to be because of land that should be there"? According to Fernando Columbus, the son and biographer of the explorer, there were also reports from the Azores that strangely carved logs and unusual boats had been found by colonists on the beaches of Flores, and that on one occasion a boat had washed ashore containing the bodies of a man and woman with broad faces "unlike those of Christians". Fernando states that his father "learned from pilots who were experienced in the voyages to Madeira and the Azores, facts and signs which convinced him that an unknown land lay to the West".

In fact, Christopher Columbus gained from Portuguese maritime tradition, much of the knowledge that drove his quest. (Indeed, there is one school of thought that Columbus was in fact Portuguese, although it is given little credence elsewhere.) He did live in Portugal for about ten years, married a Portuguese noblewoman and first attempted to propose his "Enterprise of the Indies" to King João II of Portugal. In 1484 Columbus approached the monarchs of Spain, but only after being turned down in Portugal.

The Portuguese rejection of Columbus was probably based on a number of considerations. Firstly, that there were a number of Portuguese courtiers sufficiently versed in celestial navigation and mathematics to reject the claim that the westward route to Cathay was as short as Columbus believed it to be. Secondly, Columbus's proposed "Enterprise" asked for far more generous terms than João II was accustomed to granting explorers. Columbus requested the King to finance the expedition, in variance with the usual practices pertaining to those proposing to discover Ocean islands. Thirdly, there was renewed interest in further expansion in Africa, which had revived after a decade of stagnation once João II succeeded to the throne in 1481. According to Soncino, John Cabot had also approached the King of Portugal to back Cabot's proposed voyage, although precious little is known about the circumstances surrounding Cabot's original proposal.

Gaspar Corte Real first appears in documents in 1488, at which time he was acting governor of Terceira, in the absence of his father, João Vaz Corte Real. In that same year, Bartholomew Diaz returned to Portugal from a voyage of discovery to the south, announcing that he had been successful in rounding the southern cape of the African continent, which was named "Good Hope, for the promise it gave of finding India, so desired and for so many years sought after".

The statue of Gaspar Corte Real which stands outside the Confederation Building in St. John's, a gift of the Portuguese Fishing Organization in 1965. (Ray Troke photo.)

Year-by-year, the boundaries of the known world were being pushed back. Yet, much geographical knowledge would appear to have been closely guarded, as the new trade routes were matters of considerable importance to the state. Meanwhile, it seems likely that some knowledge of Greenland was again circulating in maritime circles. There is sketchy evidence relating to many supposed discoveries of a land well to the north and west in the 1470s. According to some sources, Diddrik Pining (after 1478, the governor of Iceland) and a German navigator named Podhurst, had made one or more voyages to Greenland, as did a shadowy figure named Johannes Scolvus, in about 1476. It may be that some such voyage occurred in connection with piracy or plundering of the failing Norse settlements. Inuit legend would seem to indicate that the Norse eastern settlement finally died out around this time, partly resulting from attacks from the sea, by people who do not appear to have been Inuit. The Portuguese tradition that João Vaz Corte Real of the Azores rediscovered Greenland and North America about this time, is sometimes connected with the voyages of Pining, Podhurst, and Scolvus.

Following the successful ocean crossing of Columbus (who put into the Azores upon his return journey in 1493), the 1497 voyage of John Cabot established that there were indeed "undiscovered" lands well to the northwest of the Azores. These lands lay within the accustomed focus of Azorean exploration — for the direct route to the west seemed not feasible, because of prevailing winds and currents.

The series of voyages of exploration out of the Azores at the turn of the fifteenth century were built upon a long history of searching for islands in the Ocean Sea. These may well have been directly inspired by reports of John Cabot's discoveries. In October 1499, King João II issued a patent to João Fernandes of the Azores, to search for and discover certain islands, of which he would have the governorship if he succeeded. Fernandes may well have been the source of Azorean knowledge of the Cabot voyages out of Bristol, for he had long-standing business connections to Bristol. Thereafter, Fernandes's whereabouts cannot be determined until 1501, when he resurfaced in Bristol, in association with other Azorean Portuguese, who were engaged in voyages to the New-Founde-Land, in partnership with Bristol merchants.

A landowner, or *lavrador*, of the island of Terceira, Fernandes probably made a voyage that reached Greenland. He may have been lost on a later voyage, for after 1501 he does not appear as a member of the Bristol-Azores combine. Still later, map inscriptions noted Greenland as *Terra Labradoris*, "discovered by English of the town of Bristol… [who] gave it that name because he who gave them directions was a lavrador of the Azores''. (As the old Norse name, Greenland, was revived, the designation ''Land of the Labrador'' drifted south and was eventually assigned to the mainland, northwest of the New-Founde-Land.) Those who accept an early Azorean discovery of Greenland suggest that Fernandes may have even been a participant in the Cabot voyages.

Historian D. B. Quinn has suggested an alternative scenario for the discoveries of João Fernandes, (see plate XII) the little-known *lavrador*:

> *The most likely solution is that before 1500 (or even in 1500) he had made an overseas discovery he was not yet prepared to publicize, but that when [Gaspar] Corte Real returned with his claim to have found land, Fernandes either was forced to back down on his own claims or thought discretion better than conflict, since the Corte Real family was dominant in Terceira by this time.* [13]

The Portuguese claim to the New-Founde-Land rested on the voyages of Gaspar Corte Real and his brother, Miguel. Portugal continued for some years to be the source of European knowledge of the northern parts of the New World — previously known as the New-Founde-Land, Terra Nova, the Bacallaos, or Terra Corte Real.

Gaspar Corte Real was the third son of João Vaz Corte Real. Gaspar was described by Portuguese historian Damiao Gois (writing in the 1560s) as an ''adventurous and courageous man, wishing to gain honour… he decided to go and discover lands to the North because in the South others had already made many discoveries''. On 12 May 1500, King Manoel granted him a charter, which indicates that Gaspar Corte Real had made at least one voyage in the past, searching for new islands, ''forasmuch as Gaspar Corte Real, a

---

13   Quinn, D.B. *North America from Earliest Discovery to First Settlements: The Norse Voyages to 1612*. New York: Harper Row Publishers, 1971. p.122.

noble man of our court, has made efforts in the past, on his own account and at his own expense, with ships and men, to search out, discover and find... some islands and a mainland... ".

On his voyage in 1500, Gaspar Corte Real reached Greenland, but could not land. Where he went after that has been the subject of conjecture, because Portuguese writers, such as Gois, would seem to have confused Gaspar's two voyages. However, it appears that he may have cruised some distance north, along the west coast of Greenland, before crossing the Davis Strait. This first voyage may have included sailing to the south — possibly the rediscovery of Labrador and a coasting voyage along the northeast shore of Newfoundland.

Having made at least some discovery of land to the north and west, the next year Gaspar Corte Real put to sea again, with three caravels and support from the King. Compared to the first voyage, we have a wealth of information about the second, in the form of letters written to Italy from Lisbon by Alberto Cantino and Pietro Pasqualigo in October 1501. The expedition first tried to reach the land sighted the previous year, but:

> '*they met huge masses of solid snow floating upon the sea and moving under the influence of the waves, from the summit of which by the force of the sun's rays a clear stream of sweet water was melted and once dissolved ran down in little channels made by itself, eating its way splashingly to the base. Since the ships now lacked fresh water, the boats approached and took as much as was then needed. Fearing to remain in that region by reason of this present danger, they wished to turn back, but yet, spurred by hope, decided to go forward as best they could for a few days more, and having got under way, on the second day they again discovered the sea to be frozen, and were forced to give up the undertaking*". [from the Cantino letter]* [14]

---

14   Quinn, D.B. *New American World: A Documentary History of North America to 1612.* Vol.I. New York: Arno Press, 1979. p.148.

Corte Real then turned south and eventually discovered another land —a very large country which:

> *they approached with very great delight. And since throughout this region numerous large rivers flowed into the sea, by one of these they made their way about a league inland, where on landing they found abundance of most luscious and varied fruits, and trees and pines of such measureless height and girth, that they would be too big as a mast for the largest ship that sails the sea.* [15]

Some scholars have contended that this "large country" was Labrador, but most accept the interpretation of a sixteenth century Portuguese author that the land lay in 50°N. This latitude is approximately that of Cape St. John, at the top of the Baie Verte Peninsula. This would be a plausible landfall for a vessel approaching New-Founde-Land waters from the northeast, while "numerous large rivers... and trees... of measureless height and girth" would be consistent with a voyage into Notre Dame Bay and along the northeast coast of Newfoundland. After a lengthy coastal voyage, perhaps near St. John's and Cape Spear, Corte Real's own ship parted company with the other two caravels. Corte Real continued to explore to the south, while his companions returned to Portugal. The Pasqualigo letters cover ground much similar to that of Cantino:

> *On the eighth of the present month arrived here one of the two caravels which this most August monarch sent out in the year past under Captain Gaspar Corterat to discover land towards the north; and they report that they have found land two thousand miles from here, between the north and the west, which never before was known to anyone. They examined the coast of the same for perhaps six hundred to seven hundred miles and never found the end, which leads them to think it a*

---

15   Quinn, D.B. *New American World: A Documentary History of North America to 1612.* Vol.I. New York: Arno Press, 1979. p.148-149.

mainland. This continued to another land which was discovered last year in the north. The caravels were not able to arrive there on account of the sea being frozen and the great quantity of snow. They are led to this same opinion from the considerable number of very large rivers which they found there, for certainly no island could ever have so many nor such large ones. They say that this country is very populous and the houses of the inhabitants of long strips of wood covered over with the skins of fish [sealskins?]. They have brought back here seven natives, men and women and children, and in the other caravel, which is expected from hour to hour are coming fifty others. These resemble gypsies in colour, features, stature and aspect; are clothed in the skins of various animals, but chiefly of otters. In summer they turn the hair outside and in winter the opposite way. And these skins are not sewn together in any way nor tanned, but just as they are taken from the animals; they wear them over their shoulders and arms. And their privy parts are fastened with cords made of very strong sinews of fish, so that they look like wild men. They are very shy and gentle, but well formed in arms and legs and shoulders beyond description. They have their faces marked like those of the Indians, some with six, some with eight, some with less marks. They speak, but are not understood by anyone, though I believe that they have been spoken to in every possible language. In their land there is no iron, but they make knives out of stones and in like manner the points of their arrows. And yet these men have brought from there a piece of broken gilt sword, which certainly seems to have been made in Italy. One of the boys was wearing in his ears two silver rings which without doubt seem to have been made in Venice, which makes me think it to be mainland, because it is not likely that ships would have gone there without their having been heard of. They have great quantity of salmon, herring, cod and similar fish. They have also great store of wood and above all of pines for making masts and yards of ships. On this account his Majesty here intends to draw great advantage from the said land, as well by the wood for ships, of which they are in want, as by the men, who will be excellent for labour and the best slaves that have hitherto been obtained. This has seemed to me worthy to be notified to you, and if

71

anything more is learned by the arrival of the captain's caravel, I shall likewise let you know. [16]

Gaspar Corte Real's caravel never returned and we can only speculate as to its fate. Although we do not know for certain the size of his ship, its capacity must have been strained by having the reported 50 native passengers on board. Perhaps the fearful natives were able to overwhelm their captors at some later stage in the voyage? However, it is also possible that the vessel was lost, in a storm or during the attempt to cross the ocean.

During the following winter, Gaspar Corte Real's older brother, Miguel, organized an expedition to search for Gaspar's ship. Miguel sailed from Lisbon in May, 1502, likewise with three caravels, and with a grant from the King of the captaincy of the new lands, in confirmation of Gaspar's grant. The expedition reached the shores previously explored by Gaspar. The three caravels separated in order to widen the search, after agreeing on a rendezvous for 20 August, at a site that some have tentatively identified as St. John's harbour. In an incredible repetition of misfortune, Miguel's flagship caravel failed to appear, and there seems no doubt it was likewise lost with all hands.

The next year, the third Corte Real brother, Vasco Eanes, requested permission to search for Gaspar and Miguel. King Manoel denied the request, but appears to have sent out two ships at his own expense, returning in the fall, presumably with further news of the "Terra Corte Real", but without any news of the unfortunate Corte Real brothers, or their crews.

It has been said that the exploration of the New-Founde-Land from 1497 to 1524 is the most "dimly illuminated" episode in the rediscovery of the New World. Yet, as soon as the fishing grounds of the New-Founde-Land became known, the Portuguese, English, French and Spanish were quick to become established in this new industry. In 1501, simultaneous with Gaspar Corte Real's ill-fated

16   Quinn, D.B. *New American World: A Documentary History of North America to 1612*. Vol.I. New York: Arno Press, 1979. p.150-151.

second voyage, King Henry VII of England granted patents to a consortium of Bristol and Azorean interests, presumably for the fishery. The French were established in the new fishery by 1504, and by 1506 there were customs levied against New-Founde-Land fish by the Portuguese. It is considered likely that by this time, there were regular fishing voyages being made to the Bacallaos, out of both mainland Portugal and the Azores.

Certainly, exploration of the New-Founde-Land continued in the early 1500s. Although the locations of harbours and fishing grounds were doubtless passed along chiefly by word of mouth (as the participants had a vested interest in maintaining these trade secrets), some European maps began to show representations of the New-Founde-Land.

The earliest map that indisputably includes New-Founde-Land is the "Cantino" map of 1502. This map is named for the same Alberto Cantino whose letter about the second Gaspar Corte Real voyage is cited above. Although Cantino did not prepare the map himself, he directed its preparation and sent it to the Duke of Ferrara in Italy. The Cantino map shows a "Terra del Rey de Portugall" (land of the King of Portugal) to the southwest of Greenland. It was shown as well-wooded, with numerous islands, off a heavily-indented coastline that bears resemblance to the northeast coast of Newfoundland.

It was appropriate that the New-Founde-Land became known as a land of fish. As news of the explorations and discoveries in the southern waters began to capture the European imagination — Christopher Columbus and Amerigo Vespucci in the Caribbean and South America, Vasco de Gama in India — the New-Founde-Land seemed to be lacking in both riches and romance. Although a profitable transatlantic fishery developed almost immediately, the fishery was not altogether a pleasurable pastime.

Europe in this age was above all dominated by the aristocracy. Explorers such as Cabot, Columbus, and Corte Real had been motivated largely by their desire to join this aristocracy — to become princes of the lands discovered. It soon became clear that the land itself was of little immediate use (apart from being a source of mast trees). The "naked savages" were not amenable to being ruled over

The Portuguese White Fleet in St. John's harbour, 1970s. (Ben Hansen photo.)

While the Cantino map of 1502 (see plate XIII) does not name any of these features, by the time of the Pedro Reinal map in 1505, the Portuguese had apparently developed a nomenclature for what had become known (at least in Portugal) as "Terra Corterealis". Some of the Portuguese names applied to the southeast corner of Newfoundland where the Portuguese fishery in later years became concentrated. Other fishing nations obviously found no problem in adopting or adapting some version of the Portuguese names that are still used. Some of the earliest names remain to the present day. These include c[ape] Raso (now known as Cape Race), from the Portuguese "shaved cape"), c de espera (Cape Spear), "cape of hope", b[ay] de conceican (Conception Bay), and y dos bacallaos (Baccalieu Island). The Portuguese word for codfish, "bacallaos" was the name commonly applied by the Portuguese fishermen to the New-Founde-Land, rather than the grander, official title, "Terra Corterealis".

by a new-made prince, or to exist as either a peasantry or as slaves in their own homeland. As one early English settler noted, the common saying had it that, "fishing is a beastly trade and unseeming a gentleman."

It was left to the fishermen of Northwestern Europe, to further explore the New-Founde-Land — to the sailors of the Azores, the ports of the Portuguese mainland, and to those hardies from Bristol. It appears that, for at least a century after rediscovery, the two largest groups engaged in the new fishery of the New-Founde-Land were the Normans and the Bretons, of northern France.

5.

Sebastian Cabot, 1508-09.

"This hidden secret of nature".

A 16th-century woodcut, illustrating celestial navigation using cross-staff, quadrant, and astrolabe. (Courtesy Parks Canada.)

In 1897, on the 400th anniversary of John Cabot's discovery of the "new Isle", the Colony of Newfoundland introduced a commemorative issue of postage stamps. Then, a century ago, even more so than in 1997, a sought-after commercial advantage in celebrating the anniversary was hampered by a lack of reliable information about the voyages of Cabot, and by the absence of any authenticated image of the explorer. As Newfoundland historian D.W. Prowse had it, "Alas! for the glory of our Island, for the praise of our discoverer, there are no portraits to discuss...." On one stamp, a representation of a portrait of John Cabot's son Sebastian, was inappropriately chosen to represent "hym that founde the new Isle". Accounts of the voyages of Cabot the elder were frequently confused or combined with the accounts about, and even by, Sebastian Cabot, the son.

For many years, in accounts of the English discovery in the New World, Sebastian Cabot had been given the lion's share of the credit for John Cabot's "discoveries." Voyages made by the son in 1508-09 were consistently confused with the voyages of the father a decade earlier. And such confusion is not yet at an end, as evidenced by the garbled account in Jasper Ridley's recent *The Tudor Age* of what was purported to be John Cabot's second voyage. This work does the reverse, in crediting the father with carrying out one of Sebastian's voyages:

> *He set off on another voyage next year with the intention of getting to Japan, and sailed north from Newfoundland, entering Baffin Bay and sailing along the coast of Greenland as far as 67' ½°. He died soon after his return to England but his son Sebastian Cabot carried on, undertaking many voyages on behalf of the English.*

When Sebastian Cabot died in 1557, with England at the brink of the Elizabethan Age, he took to his grave many of the secrets of those dimly-illuminated, first years of the Age of Discovery. He was probably the last man left alive who knew with certainty what tidings had been received of John Cabot's second voyage in 1498. It is considered unlikely, but Sebastian may even have accompanied one or both of his father's expeditions. Had he done so, Sebastian could undoubtedly have helped augment the meagre details which have come down concerning the destinations and discoveries of John Cabot's voyages. He might have helped clear up much of the speculation about where John Cabot journeyed, and what he discovered.

Sebastian's knowledge could also have satisfied historians as to the nature and extent of his own voyage along the eastern seaboard of North America — presumed to have taken place in 1508-09, and itself a ''mystery voyage'' in the annals of Discovery. He would have been able to provide information on the impact of his father's discoveries on his merchant sponsors and the commerce of the port of Bristol. Such insight would also have given some inkling as to the importance assigned to the discovery of the New Isle by the British crown and on the subsequent pursuit of the fisheries off the New-Founde-Land, by the merchants of Bristol and London.

Later in his career, Sebastian Cabot was in the employ of the Spanish, and in a position to have received and recorded much of the information which was available in Europe about new discoveries. And, in his final incarnation, declaring himself once more to be an Englishman, Sebastian Cabot was a key player in the renewal of British initiatives in overseas exploration. This was a vital prelude to the Golden Age of British seamanship, during the reign of Elizabeth. Sebastian was to become the final connection to Bristol's strong involvement in the discovery of America.

When the Muscovy Company was inaugurating trade between England and Russia in the 1550s, Sebastian Cabot was ''the chief setter forth of the journey.'' He was recognized as a long-time and consistent advocate of a northern passage between Europe and Asia. Perhaps it is unfortunate that Sebastian spent his prime years, not in voyaging so much as ashore, in the employ of the Spanish, whose interests were gold and conquest, and therefore not served by Sebastian's northern theories and ambitions. His explorations in New-Founde-Land waters as a young man did prove important in establishing the continental nature of North America. However, his misleading report that he had seen open water in the far northern regions, was the starting point of series of valiant but fruitless quests after the elusive Northwest Passage and a mythical, open Polar Sea.

If a time-travelling scholar of the Age of Discovery were able to interview Sebastian in, say, 1555, he would not likely be much the wiser. Sebastian Cabot, at best, had a situational and selective memory and a tendency toward invention and misrepresentation. In his lifetime he had created a reputation as an explorer, navigator and cartographer. But, as one who made a career out of peddling his reputation to royal patrons, he made it his business to augment and adorn his own accomplishments. In short, Sebastian Cabot was a successful, lifelong blowhard — and the older he got, the harder he blew.

*   *   *

The sketchy evidence is that Sebastian Cabot was born in Venice and accompanied his parents to Spain, and then England, at a young age. He was probably a teenager during his father's two voyages to the New-Founde-Land. While there is no direct evidence that Sebastian sailed with his father in 1497 it is at least a possibility.

After his father failed to return from the 1498 voyage and was presumed dead, Sebastian continued to live in Bristol — perhaps as the young head of family in difficult circumstances. We know virtually nothing of the Cabot family in those years, when Sebastian grew into manhood. Those years must have been a major influence in shaping both his personality and his seafaring skills. It is clear that merchants of Bristol, some of whom must have been involved in the "Cabot syndicate" of 1497-98, attempted in the early 1500s to combine trading to the New-Founde-Lands with the cod fishery. They were eager to follow up on John Cabot's discoveries and his ambitions. Bristol merchants established a consortium, with the involvement of Portuguese-Azorean traders including João Fernandes. This was styled something along the lines of the Company of Adventurers into the New-Founde-Lands. Sebastian, though yet a minor, may have had some involvement with that Company. He may have represented the Cabot family's interests under the original patent issued to his father, which named John Cabot's three sons. At the very least, the Company principals such as Hugh Elyot, an associate of Cabot the father, would have kept Sebastian informed and perhaps used him as a source of information about the New-Founde-Land.

The Company of Adventurers into the New-Founde-Lands

The first attempt by the merchants of Bristol to capitalize on John Cabot's discoveries was under a charter granted in 1501 to three Bristol men and three Azoreans — including the "lavrador" João Fernandes. We have no record of their results, unless this was the voyage recorded on the Weimar map. Produced in 1530, this map identifies Greenland as being the Land of the Labrador, "discovered by the English of the town of Bristol... the one who first gave notice of it was a Labrador of the Azores."

The following year, 1531, another Bristol-Portuguese syndicate brought home a cargo of fish valued at £180 — seemingly landed under the customs exemptions granted in the 1496 letters patent. This important and seemingly profitable voyage, provides the earliest date we can establish with certainty for the beginning of the great Newfoundland fishery. Prominent among the Bristol investors in this voyage were two merchants who appear to have had a connection with both John Cabot and the Portuguese trade: Hugh Elyot and Robert Thorne.

Historian D.B. Quinn considers it most likely that any direct first-hand knowledge Sebastian Cabot had of the New-Founde-Land came from his participation in this particular voyage. When the Company of Adventurers into the New-Founde-Lands was chartered in December of 1502, Hugh Elyot was the principal adventurer. Professor Quinn suggests that the Company was in operation until 1505 or 1506, sending one or two vessels per year to the new lands from Bristol, for the purposes of both fishing and trade. Little is known of the end of the Company, apart from the series of lawsuits occasioned by its eventual collapse.

Its seems to be, that a modest exploitation of the New-Founde-Land fishery continued out of the port of Bristol, probably at the level of one or two vessel sailings each season. Maps produced in the early 1500s confirm that Portuguese vessels were also fishing the Baccallaos, on the Grand Bank of the New-Founde-Land. They were joined in 1504 by the Norman French, and in 1506 by the Bretons. By the latter year, Portugal had introduced a duty aimed specifically at Newfoundland cod. These fishery efforts prevailed throughout the 100 year Age of Discovery.

In 1505, Sebastian received a pension in his own right from Henry VII. This was for ''diligent service and attendaunce'' in and about ''our Town and poort of Bristowe'' and ''the fyndinge of the newe founde landes to our full and good pleasure.'' It is curious as to how the young Sebastian, in his early 20s, could have compiled such a record of service. Historians have speculated that this may have largely been embellishment accompanying a transfer of John Cabot's pension to his son — perhaps occasioned by the final acceptance of the father's death. Perhaps Hugh Elyot or others of the Bristol Adventurers approached the King on behalf of the Cabot family? However, it is not inconceivable that the young Sebastian was already establishing a reputation as a cartographer and navigator. And, if not directly involved in the New-Founde-Lands Company, was making other significant contributions to some overseas initiatives for the crown.

Sebastian's skill was recognized at a young age. He was considered in Bristol circles to possess some special knowledge of the New-Founde-Land, as attested by his selection in 1508 to command a new expedition. This voyage was intent upon building on knowledge of the new land already obtained from the John Cabot and Company of Adventurers voyages. It revived John Cabot's scheme of planting a ''colony'' or trading post on the new Isle; and finding a viable sea passage from the New-Founde-Land to Cathay.

There are no official accounts of that voyage. It is presumed to have begun in the spring of 1508, returning in 1509, at some time after the death of Henry VII, on 21 April of that year. Royal patronage is assumed, although not documented. One account has it that Cabot equipped two ships and three hundred men ''at his own cost'' — which seems unlikely. Whoever the patrons of the voyage were, Sebastian was directed to search for a passage to the north of the coasts discovered by his father. Accordingly, Sebastian

> *steered first for the north, until even in the month of July he found great icebergs floating in the sea and almost continuous daylight, yet with the land free by the melting of the ice. Wherefore he was obliged, as he says, to turn and make for the west. And he extended his course furthermore to the southward owing to the curve of the coastline, so that his latitude was almost that of the Straits of Gibraltar and he penetrated so far to the west that he had the island of Cuba on his left hand almost in the same longitude with himself.... These coasts... he called the Bacallaos.*

During his lifetime, Sebastian Cabot made varying claims about the extent of this voyage, most especially the degree to which he had penetrated to the north. He certainly explored the coast of Labrador, quite possibly entered Hudson Strait, and perhaps (though considered less likely) even sailed into Baffin Bay. In later years Cabot insisted that he had been at the very portals of Cathay during this northern voyage. This was, perhaps, as a result of observing the tides at the entrance to Hudson Strait, north of Cape Chidley, and assuming that these tides marked a passage. Were this discovery not sufficient for the voyage, his year-long journey may have been the first European exploration of the lands lying southwest of the New-Founde-Land, toward Florida — and the first to sail back to England using the favourable currents of the Gulf Stream.

Yet, it seems that the voyage was a commercial failure. No trading colony was founded (this would seem a major purpose, judging by the large complement of persons aboard). This was very much a follow-up voyage to John Cabot's second voyage in 1498, but again, no clear passage was established. As we now know, this last disappointment was for good reason. That there was no follow-up voyage could be attributed to the death of the Cabots' patron, King Henry VII, and the lack of interest the new king displayed in voyages of exploration. Preoccupied by European politics, it was many years before King Henry VIII chartered another voyage of discovery. And, by that time, Sebastian Cabot had wooed his way into the service of the Spanish crown.

Sebastian's willingness to switch sides led some to denounce him as a mercenary and a charlatan. But, it should be realized, the younger Cabot was acting very much in the tradition of his father. Faced with a lack of English patronage for the vision of a northern seaway to Cathay, Sebastian looked to the Spaniards for support. By virtue of discoveries and riches in central America, Spain was the leading nation in exploration of the new world.

In 1512, the Spanish government was expressing an interest in mounting an expedition "to ascertain the secret of the new land," which the Spanish called "Terra Nova". In that year, Sebastian Cabot (probably in the capacity of a map-maker) accompanied an English army to Spain for a projected invasion of France. He had interviews with colonial officials at the Spanish court. King Ferdinand soon requested that Cabot be released to the Spanish service. At this juncture England and Spain were allies, Henry VIII being married to Ferdinand's daughter, Catherine of Aragon. Cabot was given leave to return to England, collect his family and settle his affairs. He established his household in Seville and was appointed a naval captain in the Spanish service.

Sebastian Cabot was obviously considered a man of knowledge and skill by the Spanish. He was consulted by the king on colonial matters in 1514, and in 1515 was appointed ''Pilot to his Majesty''. A planned expedition ''for him to discover this hidden secret of nature'' (i.e. a passage through Terra Nova) was halted early in 1516, by the death of yet another of his royal patrons, King Ferdinand.

Once more thwarted, and this while entering into the prime of manhood (Sebastian was still in his early 30s), he had kept lines of communication open with England. An English voyage was discussed briefly in 1517 and in the early 1520s. As King Henry's chief minister, Cardinal Wolsey began to assemble support for a voyage, Sebastian was offered, as he later said, ''high terms if I would sail with an armada of his on a voyage of discovery.''

It was in connection with this voyage that the London Company of Drapers (prospective ''adventurers'' in the scheme) raised memorable objections to the employment of Sebastian Cabot as opposed to English ''maisters & mariners... having experience, and exercised in and about the forsaid Iland'' (obviously meaning, fishers in the waters of the New-Founde-Land). The Drapers urged that ships and men not be supplied

> *uppon the singuler trust of one man, callyd as we understond, Sebastyan, as we here say, was never in that land hym self, all if he makes reporte of many thinges as hath hard his ffather and other men speke in tymes past.*

When this scheme collapsed, Cabot approached a Venetian friar in London, suggesting that Venice finance a voyage in search of a passage. These negotiations also broke down and the explorer began to fear that the continued search for a sponsor would be looked at askance by his Spanish masters. Late in 1522, Cabot and the Venetian ambassador in Spain conferred and, when the ambassador revealed some knowledge of Sebastian's earlier overtures, he was begged "to keep the thing secret, as it would cost me my life."

Indeed, Sebastian was by this time, in his capacity as Pilot-Major, a high-ranking official and privy to Spanish state secrets . He had been appointed to this office in 1518, the duties of which were to provide instruction in navigation, to examine pilots, and oversee corrections to official charts. Sebastian Cabot was then the principal consultant to the Spanish government in matters relating to overseas navigation. And this in those years during which a Spanish empire was being established in South and Central America.

In 1524, a company of merchant adventurers was formed in Seville, Spain, to make a voyage to the Pacific Ocean by way of South America. The hopeful purpose was to find a more direct route than that pioneered by Magellan on his voyage of 1519-22. At least one of these adventurers had a family connection to John Cabot's voyage of 1497 — Robert Thorne the younger, son of the Bristol investor in the Company of Adventurers.

Sebastian Cabot commanded a fleet of four ships and 200 men, which sailed in April of 1526. Reaching South America, he precipitously decided to divert the expedition to the exploration of the Rio de la Plata region, to search for gold and silver. While Cabot's exploration of the South American interior did add significantly to Spanish knowledge of the area, the voyage was considered an unmitigated disaster by its backers. Cabot endured mutiny, as well as the hostility of the natives, to return to Seville four years later, in July of 1530, with but one ship out of four and only 24 men out of the original 200.

Back in Spain, Sebastian Cabot faced both criminal charges and numerous lawsuits resulting from his disastrous voyage. On the one hand, he was sentenced to banishment, although it does not appear the sentence was carried out, and on the other, he was assessed to pay heavy damages. However, he continued as Pilot-Major, although his examination of pilots was also the subject of an official inquiry in 1534. By 1538 Cabot was attending to overtures from England.

Despite questions about both his competence and veracity, in the

Cabot commemorative stamps issued
in 1897 (employing an image of
Sebastian Cabot) and 1947.

Father & Son

In 1895 Newfoundland historian D.W. Prowse condemned Sebastian Cabot, declaring "we [Newfoundlanders] have absolutely nothing to thank him for, quite the reverse." In his usual vehement style, Judge Prowse was echoing the sentiments of the scholars of his age, notably the French historian Henri Harrisse, who had taken some care in restoring John Cabot to his rightful place as the European discoverer of North America. Harrisse, and this revisionist school, relied not on the English records (which were sketchy at best and often confused the two Cabots), but on documents recently unearthed in Venice, and most especially from the archives of Simancas, in Spain.

Modern scholars seem in agreement that part of the confusion over the Cabots can be laid at the feet of Sebastian, the son. It is true that Sebastian from time-to-time implied that John Cabot's original 1497 voyage was a collaboration with his father. But, it was not until after Sebastian's death, that the garbled account preserved by Richard Hakluyt in the 1580s swept John Cabot into the background, where he remained for another three centuries. It must be remembered that Hakluyt's attempt to document the primacy of England's claim to New-Founde-Land came at a time when Sebastian Cabot, the peerless navigator, was still revered.

late 1540s, and early 1550s, the contest for Sebastian Cabot's services became an issue in Anglo-Spanish relations, particularly after Cabot finally made the move back to Bristol late in 1548. Sebastian was granted an annuity by the English in 1549 and seems to have quickly settled into a favoured role in his declining years. He became a sought-after advisor to adventurers proposing to discover a northern passage to Asia.

Cabot is known to have been consulted concerning the possibility of a northeast passage around Sweden and Russia. In 1553 he became governor of "the mystery and company of the Merchant Adventurers of the City of London... for the discovery of Cathay." The Company subsequently became both famous and prosperous as the "Muscovy Company". These adventurers initiated a profitable trade via the northern seas between England and Russia, becoming the first successful English exploring and trading company.

The last, first-hand account about Sebastian Cabot, the venerable explorer, is from the sending-off party for a Muscovy Company voyage in 1556 when the septuagenarian Cabot entertained the ship's company at an inn in Gravesend, England. It was reported that Sebastian Cabot "for very joy... entered into the dance himselfe amongst the rest of the young and lusty company." The following year Sebastian Cabot was dead, at the age of about 75 years.

On the founding of the Muscovy Company in 1553, Cabot was said to be "a man in those days very renowmed" and that moreover "the people of London... believe him to be possessed of secrets concerning English navigation." Virtually all accounts of the man mention his "secrets."

But it seems clear that the two "secrets" around which Sebastian Cabot created such a mystique, and which, for half a century were the basis for the myth of his special knowledge, were imaginings that he could never prove. They most likely were (1) the existence and location of a Northwest Passage in what is now Hudson's Strait; and (2) a method of using magnetic variation in the compass to determine longitude. In the first instance, Hudson's Strait could never become the desired Northwest Passage. As to the second secret, Cabot was not the only one to attempt the calculation of longitude from magnetic variation. But this hypothesis foundered upon one rock:

because magnetic north is not fixed, it just didn't work. Indeed, seeing as how the two great ''secrets'' which he guarded till the end of his life were false vanities, it may well be said that the only true mystery Sebastian Cabot took to his grave, was the secret of John Cabot's successors and Bristol discovery in the years 1498-1508.

It is clear that Sebastian Cabot managed to create for himself a quite considerable reputation in his lifetime. It may be as well, that he was trading on his father's reputation and achievements. Still, it seems that it was mainly after Sebastian's death that the achievements of his more obscure father, Italian navigator Giovanni Caboto, were improperly transferred to the more-renowned ''English'' master Sebastian Cabot.

6.

Giovanni da Verrazzano, 1524.
Esteban Gomes, 1525.

"All this land... is joined together".

Giovanni da Verrazzano, after a 17th century portrait.

Like John Cabot and Christopher Columbus, Giovanni da Verrazzano was Italian by birth. He had experience in the Mediterranean trade before his explorations. Like Cabot and Columbus, he dreamed of the glory and wealth to be earned in establishing a new sea route to the riches of Asia. While the Renaissance blossomed in his homeland, which was based in part on Italy's position at the centre of trade between Asia and western Europe, Verrazzano sought patronage from a monarch with a greater interest in the opening of the New World — François I, King of France.

Giovanni da Verrazzano is variously believed to have been born in about 1485, either in Florence, or to a prosperous family of Italian bankers in Lyons, France. Throughout his career, he described himself as a Florentine — a native of that northern Italian city whose merchants travelled throughout southern Europe and the Near East engaged in trade. This trade made Florence (the home of the powerful Medici family) a hub of the cultural renewal known as the Renaissance, as well as a centre of geographical knowledge, map-making and navigational science. Verrazzano appears to have learned practical seamanship in the eastern Mediterranean. He was said to be a trader, based in Cairo, during which time he is also said to have travelled extensively in Egypt and Syria.

The major contribution of Giovanni da Verrazzano to the exploration of North America was to make the first known voyage along the eastern seaboard of what is now the United States, establishing that New Spain (the previous known northern limit of which was Florida) and the New-Founde-Land were parts of the one land mass, which extended from Tierra del Fuego to Labrador. His voyage, supported by the later voyages of Jacques Cartier, also laid the basis for French claims in North America by right of discovery. However, Verrazzano is probably best known for his erroneous conclusion that a line of islands and sandbars off the coast of North Carolina was a narrow isthmus connecting the land masses of New Spain and New France. A false Sea of Verrazzano, nearly bisecting the North American continent, was pictured on many maps of the New World for years afterward.

To historians, the voyage of Verrazzano is a milestone in one other respect. This was the first exploration to North America of

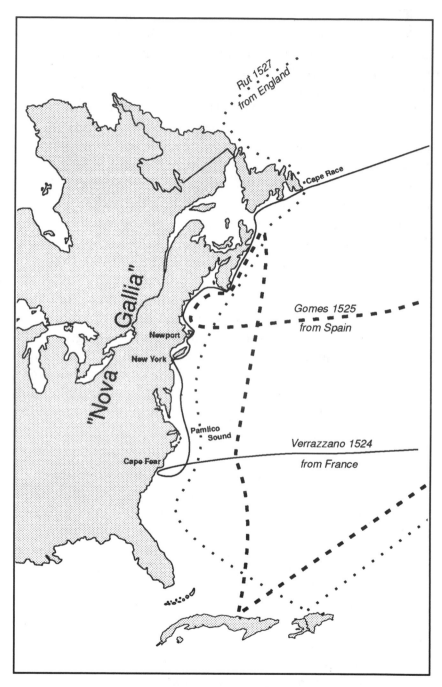

Explorations along the eastern seaboard of North America 1524-27,
on behalf of the French (Verrazzano), Spanish (Gomes), and English
(Rut) crowns. (Map by Kathy Hudson).

which there is an authentic record from the explorer himself. This was in the form of a letter outlining his discoveries, written to François I, on the return of the expedition to France. In the ten-page letter, Verrazzano describes the lands discovered, as well as their inhabitants. Fully one-third of the letter is given over to describing the appearance and habits of the natives (nowhere does he describe them as "Indians").

Insofar as it concerns any exploration of Newfoundland, Verrazzano's letter says little, for it is plain that the explorer considered his voyage of first discovery to have ended upon reaching Cape Breton when he turned for home. Thereafter he was sailing in the well-known waters of the New-Founde-Land. However, it is worth quoting the two brief passages as he approached Newfoundland:

> "After sailing CL leagues in a northeasterly direction we approached the land which the Brittani once found, which lies in 50 degrees;[17] and since we had exhausted all our naval stores and provisions, and had discovered seven hundred leagues or more of new land, we took on supplies of water and wood, and decided to return to France. Due to the lack of language, we were unable to find out by signs or gestures how much religious faith these people we found possess. We think they have neither religion nor laws, that they do not know of a First Cause or Author, that they do not worship the sky, the stars, the sun, the moon, or other planets, nor do they even practice any kind of idolatry; we do not now whether they offer any sacrifices or other prayers, nor are there any temples or churches of prayer among their peoples. We consider that they have no religion and that they live in absolute freedom, and that

---

17   Whether "Brittani" is intended to indicate "Bretons" or "Britons" is a point of contention in the debate over the landfall of John Cabot, since the "land which the Britanni once found" is, from the context of the letter, clearly Cape Breton. Both Verrazzano's letter, and his brother's map of the coasts discovered, are 4-5 degrees out in giving the "heights" of the various locales. Cape Breton is actually in about 46 degrees latitude.

everything they do proceeds from Ignorance; for they are very easily persuaded, and they imitated everything that they saw us Christians do with regard to divine worship, with the same fervour and enthusiasm that we had". [18]

"...we then left the land which the Lusitanians found long ago (that is, Bacalaia, so called after a fish)[19] and which they followed northward as far as the Arctic Circle without finding an end to it. ... In this way we find that the extension of the land is much greater than the ancients believed, and contrary to the Mathematicians who considered that there was less land than water, we have proven it by experience to be the reverse ... " [20]

It is not known when Verrazzano entered the maritime service of France, although the suggestion of some historians that he was from a French-Florentine family may indicate that it was at an early age. The earliest record of Verrazzano in France is from 1522, at which time he is identified by a report of Portuguese merchants in France, to the King of Portugal, to have been soliciting support from François I for a voyage westward to find a new sea-route to the riches of the Orient. Eventually, and with the backing of French-Florentine silk merchants and bankers at Lyons, as well as fishing and shipping interests at Dieppe, he was successful in receiving a commission from the King for his proposed voyage — the first voyage of discovery to the New World under the official auspices of the French crown.

By 1522, however, there is every indication that merchants and seamen of the northern French provinces of Normandy and Brittany

18   Tarrow, Susan. "Translation of the Cellere Codex," in Wroth, L.C. (ed.) *The Voyages of Giovanni da Verrazzano.* New Haven: Yale University Press, 1970. p.141.
19   The reference in parentheses to "Bacalaia" (Newfoundland) occurs in a marginal note, presumably in Verrazzano's hand, to the original letter. The "Lusitanians" referred to above are the Portuguese.
20   Tarrow, Susan. "Translation of the Cellere Codex," in Wroth, L.C. (ed.) *The Voyages of Giovanni da Verrazzano.* New Haven: Yale University Press, 1970. p.141

Artist Gerald Squires' conception of Beothuk pursuing seabirds off Funk Island. (Courtesy Ingeborg Marshall, photography by Manfred Buchheit.)

St. Brendan the Navigator, grounded on the back of a friendly whale, from an illuminated manuscript of the *Navigatio.* **(Courtesy Parks Canada.)**

Reconstructed Norse sod huts at L'anse aux Meadows.
(Andre Cornellier photo, courtesy Parks Canada.)

MARSOCEANUM

A portion of the 1500 Juan de la Cosa map, earlier surviving map from the Age of Discovery to show North America. West is at the top, while the "sea discovered by the English" is at top, right. (Courtesy Parks Canada.)

Henry VII of England, who rewarded John Cabot for finding the "New Isle" and supported the ill-fated voyage of 1498, as well as Sebastian Cabot's voyage in 1508. (Courtesy Parks Canada.)

A reconstruction of John Cabot's *Matthew* makes it way down the Avon River in Bristol, en route to the "new Isle," May 1997. (Curtis Rumbolt photo.)

Navigational instruments of the Age of Discovery: a half-hour glass, astrolabe, cross-staff, and compass.

Baffin Island

Leif Eiriksson 1000

Greenland

Sebastian Cabot 1508

John Davis

Labrador

Gaspar Corte Real 1500

Miguel Corte Real 1502

Giovanni da Verrazzano 15

Giovanni da Verr

New-
Founde-Land

Es

Henry Hudson 1609

Iceland

NEW-FOUNDE-LAND
at the very centre of the European Discovery & Exploration of North America

Ireland

England

John Cabot 1497

Jacques Cartier 1534

o 1524

Samuel de Champlain 1603

France

Gomes 1525

Portugal

Spain

H. Cass '97

Artist Harold Goodridge's conception of John Cabot's departure from Bristol, commissioned in 1947 by the Newfoundland Historical Society. (Courtesy the Newfoundland Historical Society and the Government of Newfoundland and Labrador.)

Pedro Reinal's map of 1501, the first to depict the New-Founde-Land as an island. In this map, which shows west at the top, the New-Founde-Land is at top, right. Cape Race (c. raso) and Cape Spear (c. esperza) are among the Portuguese placenames to have survived in Newfoundland since 1500. Note the isle of Brasil off Ireland, as well as other mythical islands. (Courtesy Parks Canada).

The Hamy King map of 1502 incorporates the earliest surviving appearance of the name Labrador — "Do Lavrador". In this map the New-Founde-Land is identified as "Bacalnaos". (Courtesy Parks Canada).

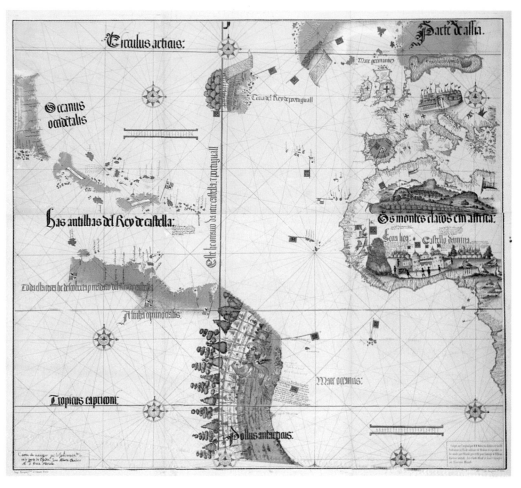

The Alberto Cantino map of 1502. The New-Founde-Land is depicted as a tree-covered island, "Terra del Rey de Portugall" —Land of the King of Portugal. (Courtesy Parks Canada).

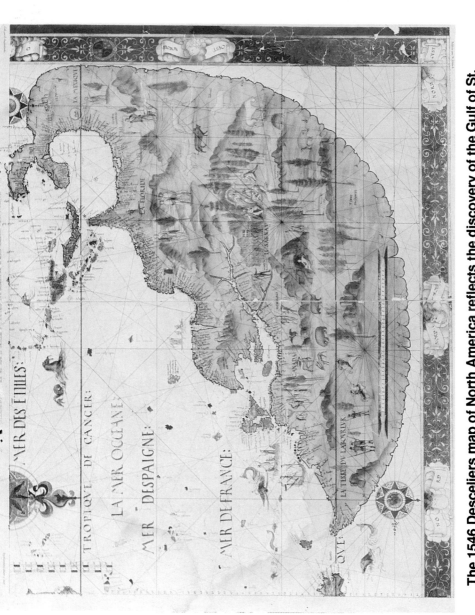

The 1546 Desceliers map of North America reflects the discovery of the Gulf of St. Lawrence by Jacques Cartier. The map is oriented with south at the top. (Courtesy Parks Canada).

As a man of enlightened thought and commercial ambition, in keeping with the atmosphere of the Renaissance and his prominent family, Verrazzano probably knew from an early age something of the exciting discoveries in the New World. The news of the expanding world became more widely known after 1506 (when Verrazzano would have been in his early 20s). The first map was printed that year showing the New World and was published by a Florentine map dealer. This was followed in 1507 by the publication in Italy of the Paesi Nouamonte, an early collection relating the voyages and discoveries of the Portuguese and Spanish.

This earliest known woodcut of a map maker at work was printed in 1598.

were familiar with the fishing grounds of the New-Founde-Land. From 1504, and probably earlier, there was a French-Breton fishery in the Baie des Chasteaux. (The Bay of Castles, our Strait of Belle Isle, was so named for the spectacular rock formations near what is now Henley Harbour. In early records, this name is applied to the whole Strait area, while Havre de Chasteaux generally applied to the inlet at the northern headland of the Strait, now known as Chateau Bay.) In 1506, a captain of Honfleur in Normandy, Jean Denys, had explored the northeast coast of Newfoundland, from Cape Bonavista to the "Golfo Castelli" — Italian for the Bay of Castles and the form of the name appearing on some early maps. Denys probably made other voyages to the New-Founde-Land, because the harbour of Renews was noted in the sixteenth century as "Havre du Jehan Denys". It is presumed, that the French and Breton fishery soon became concentrated near the Strait of Belle Isle by deliberate intention of the Portuguese, who attempted to reserve the harbours of the eastern Avalon Peninsula for themselves.

In 1508, a second French voyage of discovery under private auspices had been sponsored by Dieppe shipowner Jean Ango-the-elder. His captain, Thomas Aubert, made a voyage in that year which, in addition to fishing, was charged with discovering new fishing grounds in the New-Founde-Land. Aubert brought back the first North American Indians ever to come to France (presumably Beothuk) and recommended to Norman fishermen the fishing banks around Bonavista. Aubert's voyage is of some possible further interest in that there is some suggestion that Verrazzano may have accompanied the expedition. However, the first reference to one "Jean Verasen" as having been a member of the expedition does not appear until many years after the explorer's death.

By 1517, it would appear that the French were the dominant nation in the New-Founde-Land fishery, when John Rastell, an Englishman engaged in a fishing voyage, noted:

> Nowe frenchemen and other have founden the trade,
> That yerely of fyshe there they lade,
> Above a hundred sayle.

In the 1520s, Jean Ango-the-younger and other shipowners and

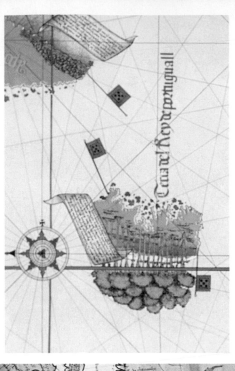

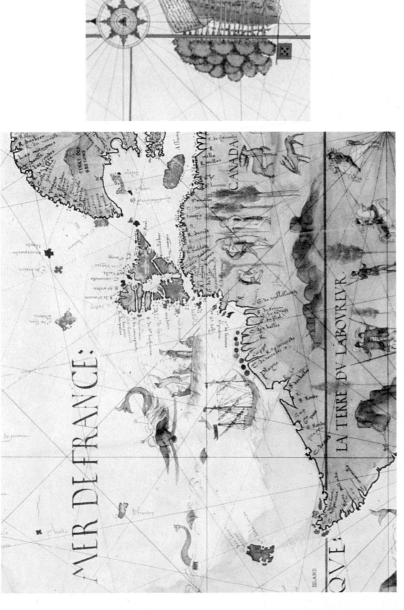

Cantino's New-Founde-Land (1502, left) compared to Desceliers' (1546, right). In the later map, Newfoundland is depicted as triangular. However, perhaps in keeping with Cartier's discovery that the "Grand Bay" was in fact a strait, the major peninsulas appear as separate islands.

top **A Dorset Eskimo soapstone quarry at Fleur de Lys;** *bottom, left* **Dorset figurines from Saglek, Labrador;** *bottom, right* **Beothuk projectile points, including a post-contact iron spearhead. (Courtesy the Newfoundland Museum).**

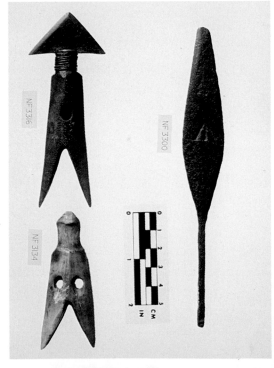

merchants of Dieppe and Rouen were sending from 60 to 90 ships each season to the New-Founde-Land. While Normandy supplied most of the ships, crews were usually found among mariners of nearby Brittany, whose expertise in the New-Founde-Land fishery was acknowledged as being without equal. This fishery was becoming an industry of some importance in northern France, with much of the capital for the fishing voyages being supplied by investors from La Rochelle, on the Bay of Biscay.

Meanwhile, others (such as Verrazzano's countrymen at Lyons in southern France) were determined that France should take its place in the New World more forcefully. Of particular interest to the bankers and silk merchants of Lyons, was the notion that the New World offered a sea route to the Orient. The discovery of this would enable them to eliminate the middlemen in their trade, having to rely on the ''Portuguese'' route around the Cape of Good Hope.

In September 1522, as Verrazzano was marshalling support for his proposed voyage of discovery, the caravel *Vittoria* limped into the Spanish port of Seville, completing the first circumnavigation of the globe. Of 250 men who had set out on the Spanish-sponsored voyage nearly three years previously, only 14 completed the journey. (One of those lost was the expedition's commander, Ferdinand Magellan, killed by a poisoned arrow in the Philippines.) This was a remarkable and notable feat but a disastrous outcome, in terms of loss of life and of ships. For once and for all, the notion that the New World was a peninsula of Asia had been put to rest and the world had been proved beyond question to be round. The true size of the globe was finally known.

Verrazzano closely considered both Magellan's achievement and his loss. It could be that Verrazzano had earlier considered participating in the voyage himself. He and Magellan had journeyed together from Lisbon to Seville in 1517 (presumably seeking support for explorations). But while Magellan's southern route to Asia certainly was regarded as too long and hazardous to be the basis of profitable trade, there was still the hope that a much shorter, more northerly sea route westwards, might be found.

What Verrazzano proposed was to head west and make land to the north of Florida — the northern limit of New Spain — and then to head along the coast, "hoping all the time to find some strait or real promontory where the land might end to the north, and we could reach the blessed shores of Cathay". To this end, he set out from Dieppe late in 1523 with four ships and 200 men, but a storm forced him to seek refuge in Brittany, two of the vessels being lost. After repairs to the two remaining ships he set out again. Skirting the Spanish coast, he received new orders and set out with but a single ship, the caravel *Dauphine*. He then made for the Madeiras, and set out across the open ocean on 17 January 1524. On 21 March 1524 — after an Atlantic crossing of eight weeks — "there appeared a new land which had never been seen before by any man". Verrazzano's landfall was in the area that now forms the border between the states of North and South Carolina, probably Cape Fear, North Carolina.

After coasting south some distance, he turned north so as "not to meet with the Spaniards" and landed near the spot where land was first sighted. The *Dauphine* proceeded north and soon Verrazzano sighted sand bars and an expanse of water beyond (Pamlico Sound), which gave flight to his hopes that he might at any moment achieve his goal of a passage. Although he did not find a breach in the narrow sand barrier, on continuing north he found a pleasant country, with many beautiful trees, which he named Arcadia (a stretch of the Virginia or Maryland coast).

Further north, Verrazzano entered a Bay which he named Santa Margarita (after François I's beloved sister), becoming the first explorer to enter what is now New York Harbour and naming the country about it the land of Angouleme— "a very agreeable place". Farther east and north, the crew rested for 15 days and replenished their supplies at "Refugio", a fine port (Newport, Rhode Island) among a beautiful and "civil" people.

Continuing east, he observed the dangerous shoals about Cape Cod. They made a final landing (probably on the coast of Maine or Nova Scotia), where the natives were not found to be nearly so welcoming, being perhaps already familiar with Europeans. The inhabitants would not allow the ship's boat to land and would only trade by sending barter items out to the boat on a rope. "We found no courtesy in them, and when we had nothing more to exchange and left them, the men made all the signs of scorn and shame that any brute creature would make (such as showing their buttocks and laughing)." Approaching the known New-Founde-Land and with his supplies running low, Verrazzano made for France.

On his return, Verrazzano reported to the King and conferred with his backers, hoping to embark almost immediately on another voyage. Late in 1524, he had another expedition ready to sail. However, a series of military defeats of the French, by the armies of the Holy Roman Emperor Charles V (also known in Spain as King Charles I) led François I to commandeer Verrazzano's ships and crew for naval campaigns. The French were defeated and François I captured at the battle of Pavia in 1525. It appears Verrazzano may have approached Henry VIII of England or Portuguese interests to back another voyage.

However, by 1526, he was again preparing to set sail under French royal auspices. The voyage was again delayed, although he made a commercial voyage to the Caribbean or Brazil. In 1528, he made another trading voyage and, on an island in the Caribbean, Giovanni da Verrazzano is said to have been killed by native Caribs and eaten within sight of his crew.

The significance of Verrazzano's contributions to knowledge of the New World was not concluded by his death. While casting about for a new royal sponsor after his voyage of 1524, Verrazzano is said to have presented Henry VIII of England with a "mightie large... mappe" and an "excellent globe" of his own making. Both have since been lost, so we have no cartographic representation of the voyage from the explorer's own hand; however, we have knowledge of two maps made shortly after the voyage. A world map by the Italian cartographer Viscount Maggiolo, dated 1527, survived until its destruction during the bombing of Milan during World War II. In 1529, Verrazzano's brother, Geralamo, also made a world map (now in the Vatican Library). There is no indication that Geralamo da Verrazzano accompanied his brother on the voyage of 1524 (although he was involved in the later trading voyages to the Caribbean). His map is presumably based upon maps and other first-hand information compiled by Giovanni.

There were doubtless many more maps of the New World made during the age of discovery than are now known to historians. The inquisitiveness of the Renaissance ensured that many of the wealthy

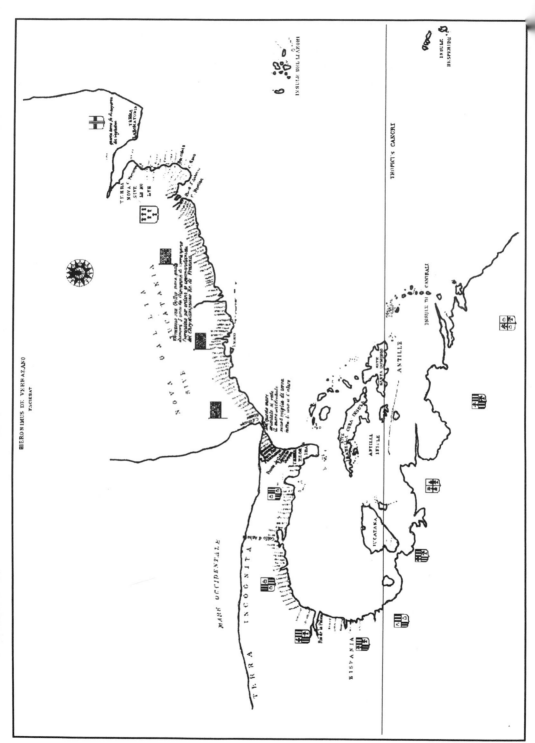

A facsimile of the North American portion of Geralamo Verrazzano's map of the world, showing the *Mare Occidentale* or Sea of Verrazzano.

acquired a map or globe to aid in their musings on the true nature of the world. Then too, geographic knowledge with respect to both the New World and the Far East changed rapidly enough that new maps were constantly required for purposes of statecraft. Traditional beliefs persisted in the representation of the new territories. As classical works of geography were read anew, the confident predictions of ancient philosophers and geographers as to the nature of the world were erroneously included in the map-maker's art.

Before he began his voyage of discovery of 1524, the maps of the New World available to Verrazzano would have shown two main parts. The largest Caribbean islands, Cuba, Jamaica and Hispaniola, had been roughly mapped, as well as a general outline of the Gulf of Mexico, the Lesser Antilles and the Spanish Main (the north coast of South America). The Florida Peninsula had not yet appeared on European maps, but Verrazzano probably knew about them through common report. His reluctance to venture into the Spanish sphere, plus comments in his letter to François I, and the Maggiolo and Geralamo da Verrazzano maps, seem to indicate that Verrazzano considered his landfall to be much farther west (and hence closer to New Spain) than it actually was. It was still not possible to accurately determine longitude.

The second part mapped, in the northwest Atlantic, presented the New-Founde-Land in 1524 either as a peninsula of Asia (which Verrazzano would have disputed even before his voyage) or as an island off by itself in the middle of a vast ocean, its coastline a maze of headlands, bays and islands. The New-Founde-Land was usually labelled either Bacalaos, Terra Nova, Terra Cortcrealis or Terra del Rey de Portugal (Land of Codfish, New Land, Land of Cortereal or Land of the King of Portugal). Between the New-Founde-Land and New Spain (south of Florida) only the ocean had been shown, seemingly promising a passage through the two new lands to Asia — the northeast coast of which was equally unknown to Europeans.

After Verrazzano's voyage, maps began to show an unbroken coastline for North America from Florida to Newfoundland — and indeed from Newfoundland to Tierra del Fuego, at the southern tip of South America. However, the pace of exploration was so swift that names that Verrazzano assigned to coastal features and his outlines of the coast were soon replaced by others.

Verrazzano's voyage for the King of France was soon followed by a Spanish-sponsored voyage, led by a native of Portugal, Esteban Gomes. Gomes had command of one of the ships in Magellan's original fleet in 1519, but had brought his ship back to Spain before Magellan headed with the other ships through the Strait of Magellan into the Pacific. Late in 1524, Gomes departed on another voyage for the King of Spain — like Verrazzano, postulating the existence of an ocean passage between Florida and the New-Founde-Land. Shortly thereafter, Spain's pilot major Diego Riberio, one of the most influential cartographers of the day, began to produce maps which, although they accepted Verrazzano's discovery of an unbroken coastline, gave the later new land the name "Tiera de Esteban Gomez", reproducing Gomes's place names and coastal features from Cape Cod to Cape Breton. Meanwhile another Spanish-sponsored exploration, by Lucas Vasquez de Ayllon, mapped the eastern coast of "Florida" north of the peninsula.

Henry VIII of England also sponsored a voyage in search of a passage shortly thereafter, which historians have speculated was inspired by the map Verrazzano had presented. In 1527, John Rut commanded an expedition of two ships, which first coasted Labrador (described as "all wilderness and mountains and woodes and no naturall ground but all mosse and no inhabitation nor no people in these parts"). Perhaps the northerly course of Rut's voyage indicates that rumours of the extent of the "Bay of Castles" were beginning to reach England. In any case, Rut did not enter the Strait of Belle Isle, but headed for a scheduled rendezvous at St. John's with the second vessel, which was presumed lost among the "Islands of ice" off Labrador. At St. John's he wrote a letter to King Henry on 3 August.

Rut then turned south, presumably under orders to continue coasting in search of a passage, and arrived in the West Indies in November. There the English were reported by the Spanish as searching for "Noruega". Noruega being Spanish for Norway, the Spanish must have supposed Rut to be considerably off course and perhaps not a little deranged. Perhaps the Rut expedition was asking after "Norumbega", which is presumed to be a place appearing on Giovanni da Verrazzano's own map. Norumbega had a long cartographical history thereafter, a mythical kingdom of plenty. After trading in the Caribbean, Rut would appear to have returned to England in the spring or summer of 1528.

Although no maps or sketches have survived from any of these voyages, it would have been unusual for explorers to return without such rough maps. The presentation of several of these early maps to various royal personages is documented. Few of these survive, presumably as they were most often hung in the royal map room and well used. Such maps were made available to royal cartographers, who also sifted other evidence such as logbooks, reports and indeed rumour in order to determine coastlines as best they could.

While the resulting maps may look odd to modern eyes, we must consider the constraints under which the explorers were operating. Attempting to chart often dangerous coasts from the heaving deck of a ship, their vision was often obscured by fog, storm or approaching nightfall. For instance, Verrazzano was neither the first nor the last explorer, in crossing what is now known as Cabot Strait, to be convinced of the existence of land to the west, indicating that Newfoundland was merely a peninsula of the New World. Additionally, there were difficulties in viewing an irregular coast, familiar to anyone who has spent time on the water. Coves, islands, peninsulas and bays all appear hopelessly jumbled together. The explorer was also at the mercy of the cartographer, as well as the engraver who produced the woodcuts or copper plates from which maps were printed. Their special art lay in producing maps that were pleasing to the eyes of customers, few of whom had any intention of using the maps to travel beyond their libraries.

It has been said that cartography, in imitation of nature, abhors a vacuum. In mapping the New World, if the interior was to be filled, map-makers had to resort to imaginative illustrations, most often depicting the cartographer's interpretation of native plant, animal and human life, uninformed by any personal experience with the new lands. Place names, too, were often cobbled together from a variety of sources. For instance, Geralamo da Verrazzano's map is notable in that place names appear evenly spaced along the entire east coast of North America. While Giovanni's place names, as known from his letter to the King, appear in approximately the right places, the spaces between have been filled with a variety of names; some presumably invented, others repetitions of names that appear elsewhere on the coast.

Cartographers were often somewhat slow to incorporate new information into their maps of the New World. Incredibly, the Italian cartographer Giacomo Gastaldi's famous map of New France (dated 1556) reflects no knowledge of Jacques Cartier's discoveries in the Gulf of St. Lawrence and the St. Lawrence River between 1534 and 1541. This map was produced supposedly to illustrate Giambattista Rasmusio's *Navigationi et Viaggi*, a collection of "navigations and voyages", which is notable in that it did offer to the public for the first time, Cartier's accounts of his second voyage. Nevertheless, Gastaldi's portrayal of a group of islands — some of which are recognizable as the Bonavista, Avalon, Burin and Northern peninsulas — is in keeping with other renderings of the coast of New-Founde-Land at this time.

The great English promoter of exploration and colonization, Richard Hakluyt, produced his first book, *Divers voyages touching the discovery of America*, in 1582 with maps by Michael Lok. Hakluyt noted that Giovanni da Verrazzano's own map and globe were among the resources used by Lok, who accordingly produced a world map that included the imagined "Sea of Verrazzano".

As mentioned, along with many of the earliest explorers, few of the names assigned by Verrazzano to the coast of North America have persisted. The single name that may be said to have lingered is Arcadia — which "drifted north" and was assigned by Samuel de Champlain to the Nova Scotia–New Brunswick area, later modified to Acadia. Verrazzano also mentioned passing an island which he noted as being similar in size to the Greek island of Rhodes. It has been suggested that, while Verrazzano's naming of this island after François I's mother ("Aloysia") disappeared, his comparison persisted and the name Rhode Island has survived.

As neither Gomes, Ayalla nor Rut found any sign of the Sea of Verrazzano, the explorer's reputation undoubtedly suffered in maritime circles. Yet the Sea of Verrazzano and several of his place names continued to be employed by some cartographers — chiefly his fellow Italians, who presumably would have had access to his records. Meanwhile, it was only a few years after Verrazzano's death that another French voyage was able to "detach" Newfoundland from the rest of North America once again — that of Jacques Cartier.

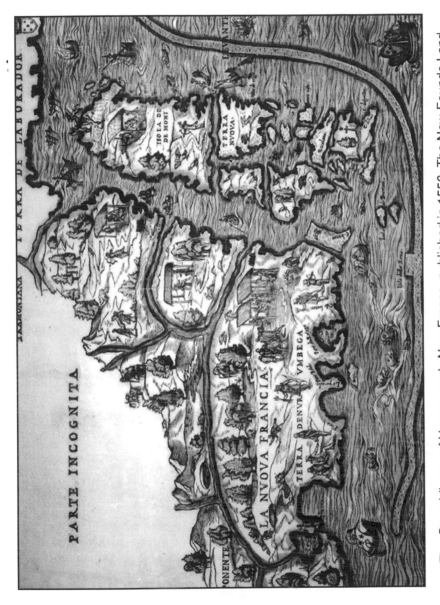

The Gastaldi map of Verrazzano's New France, published in 1556. The New-Founde-Land is shown as an archipelago. (From the National Map Collection, National Archives of Canada.)

This map was produced in 1612, by which time the New-Founde-Land was known to be a island, roughly triangular in shape. (From the National Map Collection, National Archives of Canada.)

As to the place of Verrazzano in the exploration of New-Founde-Land, it might again be said that his mistakes were as influential as his discoveries. For not only did his voyage proclaim a non-existent sea, it erroneously concluded that the New-Founde-Land and New Spain were a part of the same land: "All this land or New World which we have described above is joined together. ..." Soon after his voyage, earlier depictions of the New-Founde-Land as an island mistakenly gave way to maps that showed an unbroken coastline.

7.

Jacques Cartier, 1534, 1535-36, & 1541-42.

"The best fishing possible".

A model of Cartier's flagship *Grand Hermine*. (Courtesy Parks Canada).

Historian D. B. Quinn has written of Jacques Cartier that for "speed, competence and certainty… [he] set a new standard in North American discovery and one which was rarely surpassed." Of the European explorers who frequented Newfoundland waters in the Age of Discovery, Cartier is one of the few to have survived his explorations. He avoided the fate of John Cabot, the Corte Reals, Henry Hudson, and Sir Humphrey Gilbert — each of whom fell victim to the very seas they set out to explore. He also fared better than Giovanni da Verrazzano and John Davis who were both killed by natives of the new lands they were exploring (albeit far from Newfoundland waters).

The voyages of Jacques Cartier clearly illustrate the great importance of Newfoundland and Labrador as the hub of all European discovery and exploration of North America. His voyages of 1534 and 1535-36, made with the intention of expanding France's knowledge of and claim to the New World, were rooted in the New-Founde-Land fishery and the French experience in, and knowledge of, Newfoundland and Labrador waters.

Cartier's three voyages of exploration were usually considered, in Canada, to comprise the "discovery" of Canada as it existed before the confederation with Newfoundland. Indeed, it was Cartier who applied the Iroquois word *kanata* (village) to the country between Quebec and Montreal. His explorations made known the St. Lawrence River — a route into the interior of the North American continent — and for the first time, introduced the vastness of that interior into the European knowledge.

Jacques Cartier's voyages (along with the earlier voyage of Verrazzano) established a grand claim to a "New France", which would later be exploited by the French, to challenge Spanish domination of the New World. A second "discovery" of Cartier, was a major defining characteristic of Canada: twice he over-wintered in the vicinity of what is now Quebec City, making known the severity of the Canadian winter.

One key factor in securing Jacques Cartier's place in history is the extensive written record of his first two voyages. Of his third voyage in 1541–42, we have only a fragmentary account.

Virtually every Canadian has some knowledge of Cartier as the "discoverer of Canada." However, it is the detailed account of the Breton pilot's first voyage that provided the best available early descriptions of Newfoundland and Labrador. That voyage of 1534, made known the extent of the "Bay of Castles" (the Strait of Belle Isle) and the "Grand Bay" (the Gulf of St. Lawrence). While returning from his second voyage in 1536, Cartier became the first to pass through "Breton Strait" (now known as Cabot Strait) and established the vital fact that the New-Founde-Land was separated from the North American mainland and was, in fact, an island.

It must be said, that while Cartier made better known the great potential of the fishery in Newfoundland and Labrador waters, his characterization of the land itself was not favourable. Certainly, his often-quoted description of Labrador was almost wholly negative: "I did not see one cart-load of earth and yet I landed in many places... there is nothing but moss and short, stunted scrub. I am rather inclined to believe that this is the land God gave to Cain."

As with so many of the explorers who sailed into New-Founde-Land waters, Jacques Cartier's earlier life is almost unknown. His family may well have been fishermen and mariners. Although portraits of the explorer appear in many works on Canadian history, we do not really know what he looked like, for there is no portrait in existence that was painted while he was alive.

Left, a conventional portrait of Jacques Cartier, from Prowse's *History*. Right, a representation of the explorer from a contemporary French map, which may have been drawn from life.

However, the various posthumous portraits of Cartier do have some things in common: strong features, a particularly prominent chin and a short beard.

We know that Cartier was born in St. Mâlo, Brittany, (at that time an independent duchy, Brittany was not joined to the French crown until the 1550s). Like many Malouins, he became a mariner at an early age. His marriage in 1520 to Catherine des Granches improved his prospects, because his wife's family was both well-known in business and respected in St. Mâlo. It has been surmised that Cartier may even have sailed on the voyages of Verrazzano in 1524 and 1528. By 1532, Cartier was a navigator of considerable reputation, in a community that was known throughout France for producing the most able mariners.

The town of St. Mâlo was named after its founder, a seagoing, Celtic monk who was a contemporary of St. Brendan of Ireland. St. Mâlo is quite picturesque, being built at the end of a small peninsula, jutting into the sea. Surrounded by rocks, reefs and small islands, the town of St. Mâlo always had, as its main business, the training of seamen. Right into the 1990s it was still the major port for the French fishery off the islands of St. Pierre and Miquelon and on the Grand Banks of Newfoundland. Historically, St. Mâlo has long served as a hiring-port for the fisheries of northern France, with many of the fishermen being recruited from among the peasant population of surrounding villages.

Generally, little is known about the ordinary crewmen on voyages of discovery to the New World, such as those made by Jacques Cartier. Probably Cartier was more fortunate than most, in crewing his expeditions, for he recruited in his hometown and thus had a large proportion of experienced fishermen. Some of his seamen would have had experience in New-Founde-Land waters, prosecuting the French fishery at the Bay of Castles (the Strait of Belle Isle). Various members of the crew would appear to have been familiar with locations for taking on birds for fresh meat, as well as wood and water.

Before Cartier's first voyage, it was found necessary to issue a proclamation delaying the departure of the fishing fleet from St. Mâlo until the crew list had been filled.

For voyages of exploration, seamen were usually paid at rates comparable to those paid in the Royal Navies: for the French 6 livres, 5 sous per month; for the English 6 shillings. This was only slightly more than was needed to pay for each sailor's monthly provisions aboard ship. "Gromets" or ship's boys, who would graduate to able seamen after one voyage, were paid slightly less. The ship's carpenter or caulker and the bosun (who transmitted the master's orders to the crew and had a special responsibility for the ship's boats and the training and supervision of the ship's boys) received slightly more than the able seaman. Officers would usually include a captain and a navigator (although Cartier filled both those offices), as well as a master for each additional vessel. The backers of the voyage would also appoint a "supercargo" to account for their investment. In addition to greater pay, the officers, supercargo, and probably the barber-surgeon, would expect to be supplied with wine, fresh bread and fresh meat — at least in the early stages of the voyage.

Prior to the discovery of the fishing grounds off the New-Founde-Land, the focus of the French fishery was off the Atlantic coast of France, with cod and mackerel being important species. There were also fisheries for salmon and carp in the larger French rivers, such as the Seine and Loire. The major offshore fishery out of French ports exploited the European, North Sea herring stocks. To a large extent, this herring fishery was conducted out of ports in Normandy.

It has always seemed curious to seafaring Newfoundlanders that an explorer such as Cartier should be hailed as a "discoverer", when the waters he and his contemporaries were sailing into on these voyages. were already being fished each year by crews from England, France, Spain, and Portugal.

The Norman French were fishing in waters off the New-Founde-Land as early as 1504. They were closely followed by the Breton French, who appear to have become dominant in these new fisheries by 1515. After the fishery had become transatlantic, Dieppe and Rouen continued to be the major centres for shipbuilding and ship-owning. Yet, even for the established fishing fleets of Normandy, there was a preference for hiring skilled pilots and seamen from nearby Brittany.

As religious rulings multiplied the number of "fast days" when the eating of meat was prohibited, fish became an essential requirement for food to Roman Catholic France. By the mid-1600s (including the 40 days of Lent), there were 166 such fast days in the year. France was the most populous country of Europe by a wide margin and the home demand and market for fish was considerable. But vessels from ports such as St. Mâlo also transported and sold large quantities of cod to Italian markets, because the fishery in the Mediterranean was of little consequence.

New-Founde-Land cod had one great advantage over herring: its ease of handling. Herring had to be kept in its pickle and transported in barrels. Dried cod was customarily sold by the "little hundred" (110 fish) or the "thousand" (by custom, 1200 fish) and could be stored or transported relatively easily.

Although local demand varied according to local tastes, cod was generally held to be much tastier than herring and allowed for greater variety in cooking. Breton methods of cooking dried cod were, and are, remarkably more varied than the traditional Newfoundland "feed" of boiled salt fish and potatoes, or brewis. The rocky shore that connected the peninsula of St. Mâlo to the mainland, *Le Sillon*, (The Wake), had been set aside for the drying of fish as early as 1519—for much of the cod caught by the French was transported back to the mother country "wet" or green (meaning salted, but not dried).

By 1532, the French fishery in Newfoundland was well established. In Normandy and Brittany, there were many with day-to-day knowledge of at least this part of the New World, compiled over many fishing seasons. In particular, the Bretons had traditional fishing grounds and established transatlantic routes to the "Baie de Chasteaulx" (the Bay of Castles, or the Strait of Belle Isle, between the northern tip of Newfoundland and southern Labrador). As more fishing vessels made the journey, it became known that the Bay of Castles widened into what we now know as the Strait of Belle Isle. This expanse of sea, known then as the "Grande Baie," roughly corresponded to the northern part of the Gulf of St. Lawrence.

As France began to recover from the military setbacks of the mid-1520s, commercial interests in the north of France began to suggest further voyages of discovery to the northern coasts of the

Henley Harbour, Chateau Bay (the Bay of Castles) as depicted by the Rev. William Grey in the nineteenth century.

New-Founde-Land, to establish French claims to new fishing grounds and to investigate other potential sources of profitable trade. Moreover, the southwestern limits of the Grand Bay (Gulf) had not been established.

As the French King, François I, and the state recovered from the defeat of France by the arms of the Hapsburgs in 1525, the King began to consider new ways to recover his stature and his ransom — and to tweak the long nose of Charles V, King of Spain, and the Hapsburg Holy Roman Emperor. This tended to make François I receptive to new ventures in the New World. In 1532, while on a pilgrimage to Mont-Saint-Michel in Brittany, Abbott Jean le Veneur urged him to consider an expedition. The Abbott, who was also Bishop of St. Mâlo and may have been a relative of Cartier, followed up the meeting with a letter to the King, recommending Jacques Cartier's skills and experience in previous voyages to Brazil and

New-Founde-Land. However, we have no record of when such prior voyages had taken place, or under whose patronage.

King François I was sufficiently interested that, while on a pilgrimage to Rome in 1533, he consulted on the matter with Pope Clement VII. He obtained the Holy Father's opinion that the Papal Bull of 1493, which had divided the New World between Spain and Portugal, applied only to lands that were known in the year that the Bull was issued. With this last, major complication removed, François I agreed to sponsor a new voyage of discovery.

Jacques Cartier received a charter and commission for a voyage of discovery early in 1534. The King agreed to supply and provision two ships of about 60 tons each, crewed by 61 men in total. Cartier set out from St. Mâlo on 20 April 1534 and made the ocean crossing in 20 days, making landfall at Cape Bonavista. Whatever the status of Cape Bonavista as the fabled "landfall of Cabot", it was apparently the usual landfall for ships sailing from northern France. With some experience in voyaging to New-Founde- Land, Cartier would appear to have unhesitatingly made for Cape Bonavista, which lies in latitude 48°42'N — by Cartier's reckoning, 48°30'. St. Mâlo lies in latitude 48°39'N and sailors of the age, when they could, sailed along familiar lines of latitude from a point of departure. This fact partially accounts for New-Founde-Land being the invariable destination of European explorers. The abundance of fish surrounding Newfoundland also caused the fishery fleets to uniformly target these waters.

Cartier, fearing that his vessels might be damaged by icebergs, that were always a hazard around the Cape in spring, put in at St. Katherine's Harbour (now known as Catalina), where he spent ten days "waiting for time" and rigging and fitting out the ship's longboats for exploration. Cartier's longboats were to do yeoman service in his voyages, as he followed the prudent practice of anchoring his ships outside of unknown harbours, while the longboats took soundings and tested the holding ground for anchorage. It was a testimony to his previous experience with the treacherous waters of both Brittany and Newfoundland, that the Cartier expeditions were to enter and explore more than 50 previously undiscovered harbours and bays in the Gulf of St. Lawrence without serious mishap.

In the early stages of his voyage, sailing off Newfoundland, Cartier was frequenting harbours that were known and named. He was following a well-known track, and one with which he had some personal experience. On rounding Cape Bonavista, he made directly for the Isle of Birds (Funk Island) in order to reprovision. The description of Funk Island in the account of the voyage is worth quoting at length:

> *And on the twenty-first of the said month of May we set forth from this harbour [Catalina] with a west wind, and sailed north, one quarter northeast of Cape Bonavista as far as the Isle of Birds, which island was completely surrounded and encompassed by a cordon of loose ice, split up into cakes. In spite of this belt, our two longboats were sent off to the island to procure some of the birds, whose numbers are so great as to be incredible, unless one has seen them; for although the island is about a league in circumference, it is so exceeding full of birds that one would think they had been stowed there. In the air and round about are a hundred times as many more as on the island itself. Some of these birds are as large as geese, being black and white with a beak like a crow's. They are always in the water, not being able to fly in the air, inasmuch as they have only small wings about the size of half one's hand, with which however they move as quickly along the water as the other birds fly through the air. And these birds are so fat that it is marvellous. We call them apponats [great auks], and our two longboats were laden with them as with stones in less than half an hour. Of these, each of our ships salted four or five casks, not counting those we were able to eat fresh. ...*
>
> *Furthermore, there is another smaller kind of bird that flies in the air and swims in the sea, which is called godetz [murres, commonly known in Newfoundland as turrs]. These stow and place themselves on this island underneath the larger ones. There were other white ones larger still that keep apart from the rest in a portion of the island and are very ugly to attack, for they bite like dogs. These are called margaulz [gannets]. Notwithstanding that the island lies 14 leagues from shore, bears swim out to it from the mainland in order to feed on these*

*birds; and our men found one as big as a calf and as white as a
swan that sprang into the sea in front of them. And the next
day, which was Whitsuntide, on continuing our voyage in the
direction of the mainland, we caught sight of this bear about
half way, swimming towards land as fast as we were sailing;
and on coming up with him we gave chase with our longboats
and captured him by main force. His flesh was as good to eat
as that of a two-year-old heifer.* [21]

GREAT AUK.

Great auks, as depicted on the Grand Banks in the 1689 *English
Pilot.*

*Cartier's note that the Breton fishermen called the great auks apponats is of
interest, for this would appear to be the Beothuk word for these now-extinct,
flightless seabirds. Cartier, or his seamen, had obviously conversed with
the native Indians, the Beothuk, who regrettably are also now extinct.
Cartier's second voyage also stopped at Funk Island and the account of
that voyage suggests that "This island is so exceeding full of birds that all
the ships of France might load a cargo of them without one perceiving that
any had been removed." The last great auks on Funk Island were killed by
1800 and the species became extinct in 1844. Funk Island's murre and
gannet colonies have recovered spectacularly since it was made a seabird
sanctuary in 1964.*

21   Ramsey Cook (ed.). *Voyages of Jacques Cartier.* Toronto: University of
     Toronto Press, 1993. p.4-5.

On 27 May, Cartier reached Quirpon, on the northern tip of Newfoundland, where he again thought it prudent to wait for the ice to move off and better weather. His account takes note of an island within the harbour, now known as Jacques Cartier Island. On 9 June, he rounded Cape Bauld, on the northern tip of Newfoundland, and entered the Bay of Castles, crossing the Strait to Chateau Harbour, on the southern coast of Labrador. The expedition then proceeded west up the Labrador coast and explored along the Quebec Lower North Shore for some distance before crossing the Strait to the Newfoundland side at Cap Double (Point Riche). At one harbour, well inside the Grand Bay, (Gulf of St. Lawrence), he encountered a fishing vessel from La Rochelle, which he helped guide back to ''Brest'' (Bonne Esperance) or Good Hope.

Cartier then entered *terra incognita*, coasting from Point Riche to Cape Anguille, on the west coast of the New-Founde-Land. He was the first explorer to describe the west coast and he named the features as he went along. In each instance, the account of the voyage gives reasons for the names assigned (in honour of the Saint's day on which some cape or bay was discovered, or else descriptive of the feature named). Unfortunately, none of his place names have survived in Newfoundland.

Indeed, in the part of Newfoundland where the most names of Breton origin have endured (the north coast of the Old French Shore, at the tip of the Great Northern Peninsula) many placenames, such as DeGrat and Quirpon, would appear to have been established by the time of Cartier's visit. Other placenames of Breton origin in this area include Cremailliere, Brehat, Griquet, Fischot and Cape Rouge. They have endured because this was one area in Newfoundland where the English fished alongside the French. The saints favoured by the Bretons also gave their names to many harbours. Some of these, such as St. Anthony and St. Lunaire, were indeed applied by Cartier to harbours within the Gulf of St. Lawrence, but if the Newfoundland harbours bearing these names were named by Cartier, (as local tradition has it) that must have occurred during the poorly-documented, third Cartier voyage, when he laid up at Quirpon once more, and for some time.

Along the coast southwest of Point Riche, Cartier noted the Long Range Mountains, which he named *Les Monts des Granches*. This

122

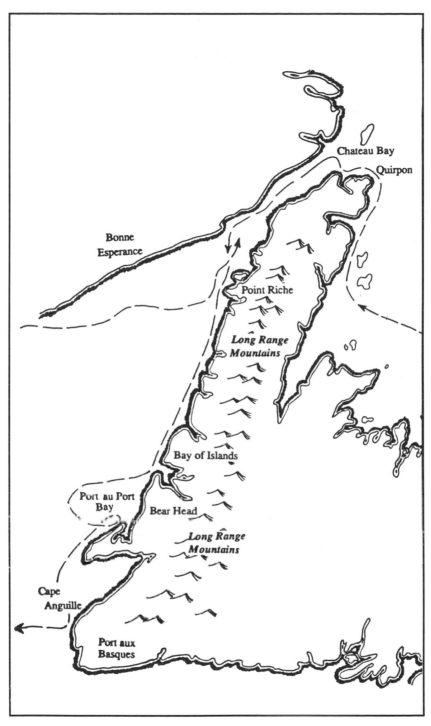

Cartier's route along the west coast of Newfoundland in 1534.
(Map by Kathy Hudson).

translates as "Barn Mountains" after their shape, but the name was probably given in compliment to his wife's family name, des Granches. There is some linguistic similarity between *Les Granches* and Long Range, but this is probably a coincidence.

To return to the translation of Cartier's journal:

> *These highlands and mountains are cut up and hewn out; and between them and the sea are low shores. On the day before this we had had no further sight of the coast on account of the fog and thick weather we experienced. And in the evening we caught sight of a break in the coast line, like the mouth of a river, between the said Barn Mountains and a cape that lay to the south-southwest of us some three leagues off. This cape is all eaten away at the top, and at the bottom towards the sea is pointed, on which account we named it the Cap Pointu [Cow Head]. To the north of it, one league off, lies a flat island.*

> *And as we wished to examine this opening, to see if there was any good anchorage and a harbour, we lowered the sails for the night.*

> *The next day, the 17th of June, we had a storm from the northeast, and we clewed up the mainsail to scud before it and housed the topmasts. We ran some 37 leagues in a southwesterly direction until Thursday morning, when we came abreast of a bay full of round islands like dovekies, and on this account we called them Les Coulonbiers [The Dovekies] and the bay, Baie de Sainct Julian [now known as the Bay of Islands]. From this bay to a cape that was named Cap Royal [Bear Head] lying to the south, one quarter southwest, the distance is seven leagues. And to the west-southwest of this cape there is another cape, which is much worn away at the bottom and round at the top, to the north of which about half a league there lies a low island. This cape was named Cap Latte [Cape Cormorant — the "low island" noted is L'Isle Rouge, for many years afterward the hub of the French fishery on the west coast of Newfoundland]. Between these two capes are low shores, beyond which are very high lands with apparently rivers among them. Two leagues from Cap Royal there is a depth of*

124

20 fathoms and the best fishing possible for big cod. Of these cod we caught, while waiting for our consort, more than 100 in less than an hour.[22]

The longboats then entered Port au Port Bay and determined that it was land-locked at the south end and proceeded around Cape St. George, sighting another "island", which Cartier named for St. John (probably Cape Anguille). Cartier then steered west into the Gulf of St. Lawrence, noting the currents and suggesting that "I am rather inclined to believe from what I have seen that there is a passage between Newfoundland and the Breton's land [Cape Breton]. If this were so, it would prove a great saving both in time and distance, should any success be met with on this voyage".

The first voyage continued, exploring what we now know as the Magdalen Islands, Prince Edward Island, the Bay de Chaleur, Gaspé, Anticosti Island and the north shore of the Gulf of St. Lawrence. Cartier did not realize that they had crossed the mouth of the St. Lawrence River. Cartier and his crew traded for furs with the Micmac and, at Gaspé Harbour, met with a group of Iroquois, who had come from the area around what is now Quebec City, for a summer fishery. Two sons of the chief, Donnaconna, were taken back to France to train as interpreters for future voyages. By 15 August, Cartier was again in Chateau Harbour and then set out on the voyage back to St. Mâlo.

His discovery of a new inland sea (seeming to offer the best chance of a passage through the New World) and the promise of an extensive new country, quickly gained Cartier the support of the admiral of Britanny, Philippe Chabot. Almost immediately the further patronage of the King of France was also secured (he pledged 3000 *livres* in October 1534). An expedition to follow up the new discoveries was planned for the following spring. This time, Cartier was to have three ships and 110 men.

This second voyage was the best-known of Cartier's explorations.

---

22 Ramsey Cook (ed.). *Voyages of Jacques Cartier*. Toronto: University of Toronto Press, 1993. p.10.

A 19th-century skiff (similar to the longboats employed by Cartier) probes an inlet into the "Barn Mountains" on Newfoundland's west coast.

He sailed, following the directions of his two Indian guides, to the "mouth of the great river of Hochelaga and the route towards Canada" (the St. Lawrence River), built a base camp near Donnaconna's village of Stadacona (present-day Quebec City), made a visit to Hochelaga (Montreal) and absorbed many fanciful and wonderful tales of the fabled land of the Saguenay — a mythical country to the north and west, which Donnaconna's people claimed to be both wealthy and civilized.

When Cartier returned to Stadacona from Hochelaga (see plate XIV), he found his men building a fort. Relations with Donnaconna's people had begun to deteriorate. Mistrust and misunderstanding continued to mount over the course of a harsh winter. Of Cartier's crew, 25 died during the winter, mostly of scurvy, before Donnaconna's people showed them a cure made from the bark from trees. Once navigation opened up in May 1536, Cartier kidnapped Donnaconna and left, carrying, in addition to a few furs, several pieces of "gold".

On his return trip to France, Cartier decided to test his theory that there was a strait between Newfoundland and Cape Breton. In early June, he determined that this was in fact the case. He crossed from Cape Breton to Newfoundland, where he rested in a harbour which he called Hable du Sainct Esperit ["Harbour of the Holy Ghost", likely the present "Port aux Basques"]. Before crossing the Atlantic to St. Mâlo he stopped at St. Pierre, off the South Coast of Newfoundland, "where we met several ships both from France and from Brittany" and finally took on wood and fresh water at Rougnouse [Renews], on the east coast of Newfoundland's Avalon Peninsula.

In St. Mâlo and Paris, the reception accorded his return was very enthusiastic. On receiving Cartier's report, François I awarded Cartier ownership of the *Grande Hermine*, a ship which the King had supplied for the voyage. However, plans to resume exploration were put on hold, as King François had again become embroiled in war with Charles V of Spain.

It was not until 1541 that the King ordered a new, and very large, expedition, in concert with a colonizing effort, that was to be headed by Jean-François de la Rocque de Roberval. The biggest expedition

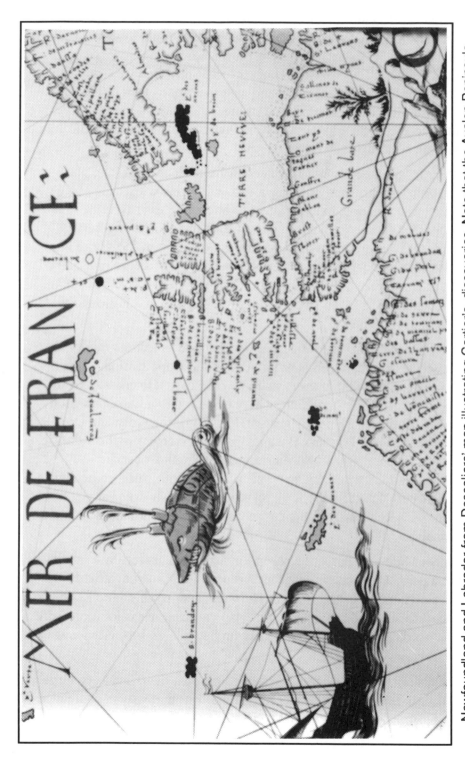

Newfoundland and Labrador from Desceliers' map illustrating Cartier's discoveries. Note that the Avalon Peninsula and the "southwest corner" of Newfoundland are depicted as separate islands. This map was produced with north at the bottom, contrary to the usual modern practice.

of the three Cartier voyages, unfortunately we have only sparse documentation in comparison with the first two. That is a great pity, because there certainly was intrigue and adventure aplenty. One of the most exciting events was played out at St. John's harbour, where the returning Cartier finally met up with the much-delayed Roberval, in the summer of 1542. Despite orders from Roberval to return to Canada with the colonists, Cartier slipped out of St. John's under cover of darkness, believing that he had in his possession a cargo of gold and diamonds, which, to his immense embarrassment and disappointment, turned out to be iron pyrites and quartz.

Although a special commission of inquiry held in 1544 found that Cartier had been a faithful trustee of the King's monies, thereafter, he was largely discredited, and never again entrusted with any charter for exploration. In 1545, an account of the second voyage appeared, while the account of the first voyage was not published until 1565. After his three voyages, Cartier would appear to have concentrated on business and on building his estate near St. Mâlo. He died on 1 September 1557, at the age of 66 years, possibly falling victim to the deadly influenza epidemic that swept Europe in that year.

8.

Martin Frobisher, 1576-78.
Sir Humphrey Gilbert, 1583.
John Davis, 1585-87.
Samuel de Champlain, 1603-15.
Henry Hudson, 1609-10.

"The only thing left undone".

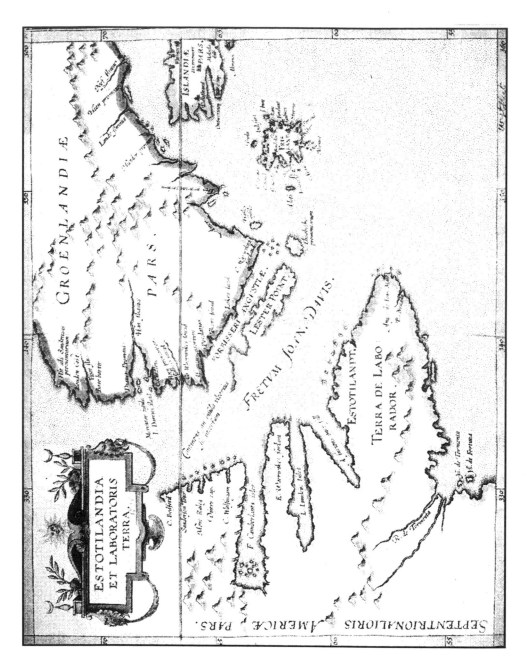

This 1598 map documents the explorations of John Davis and also incorporates elements of the Zeno hoax, including the mythical Frisland and the title "Estotilandia." The map also incorporates Davis's misconception that Frobisher's Strait (*Forbisseri Angustlae*) was a true strait through southern Greenland. (Courtesy the Centre for Newfoundland Studies.)

Although Newfoundland was rediscovered under the auspices of the English crown in 1497, for the century that followed, England was only one of four nations involved in the New-Founde-Land fishery — and, at that, lagged well behind France, Spain and Portugal. The growth of English sea power, and the advance of England from being a minor player to a position of dominance in the New-Founde-Land fishery, occurred during the reign of Queen Elizabeth I. During the Elizabethan era, there was dramatic expansion of both English sea power and maritime trade. One result of England's becoming officially Protestant (under Elizabeth's father, Henry VIII) was that the nation no longer considered itself bound by papal edicts, including those that had divided the New World between Spain and Portugal.

Particularly in the county of Devon, a new generation of high seas mariners was emerging — thoroughly professional seamen and expert navigators. One example of this Elizabethan seamanship is found in the career of John Davis, whose life was dedicated to exploration, the science of navigation and the service of his Queen and Country. Davis was born about 1550, near Dartmouth, Devon. Devon, and the neighbouring county of Dorset in the English West Country, were to play the leading role in expanding England's interest in the New-Founde-Land and consequently supplied much of the personnel for the Queen's Navy.

Although little is known of Davis's early life, it is presumed that he had a youthful interest in maritime pursuits, as did several of his childhood neighbours. Most notable among these neighbours were the Gilbert family, whose ancestral home was in sight of Sandridge, the Davis family's freehold. Davis seems to have been a lifelong friend and confident of Adrian Gilbert, who was about the same age. His career was also helped by his connections with Adrian's better-known siblings — his older brother, Humphrey Gilbert, and his younger half-brother, Walter Raleigh.

John Davis first appears in documents in 1579, at which time he was already a highly regarded mariner in the West Country ports of Dartmouth and Exeter. The next year, Davis and Adrian Gilbert were mentioned in the journal of Dr. John Dee — one of the leading mathematicians and cosmographers of the day, and a man of some influence at court. In all likelihood, Gilbert and Davis were seeking support for the schemes of Adrian's older brother, now Sir Humphrey Gilbert, who was circulating proposals to increase the English influence in the New World by colonization and exploration (his 1577 tract was titled *A discourse how hir Majestie may annoy the King of Spayne*). Shortly thereafter, Davis was married to a daughter of Sir John Fulford, providing another connection in Devon maritime circles — with another family more influential than Davis's relatively humble one.

From the 1560s, such notable Devonshire seafarers as John Hawkins and Francis Drake had been steadily pushing a build-up of the English Navy. They sought to prey upon the Spanish treasure ships from South America, to "annoy" the King of Spain, and to defend Protestant England from the ambitions of the Catholic monarchs of the continent. Despite the important early role played in maritime affairs by the port of Bristol, the English-Newfoundland fishery was also becoming the particular "stay and support" of the West Country. The potential of this fishery as a "nursery for seamen" experienced on the high seas was recognized as vital for Britain to "rule the waves". Legislation was passed to encourage the industry — through increasing the number of fish days in the week and by imposing duties on all foreign-caught fish.

From about 1580, international tensions made for a further emphasis on interest in naval matters and in the New-Founde-Land. Privateering was beginning to get out of hand, further contributing to strained relations between England and Spain. Writing in 1578, mariner and trader Anthony Parkhurst noted of the fishery that the English presence was increasing yearly, but still lagged well behind the fisheries of France and Spain. One of Parkhurst's suggestions was that the English could take and fortify the Strait of Belle Isle "and from thence send wood and cole with all necessaries to Labrador, lately discovered". Unlike the more populous and catholic maritime nations of continental Europe, England's home fishery was able to supply domestic demand. The New-Founde-Land fishery was nevertheless seen to be an important asset for England. The strategic importance of the fishery lay in the role played by dried cod for supplying armies in the field and ships engaged in overseas trade. As mentioned, the sailor-fishermen were seen to be of great value to man Britain's naval vessels on short notice, in event of war.

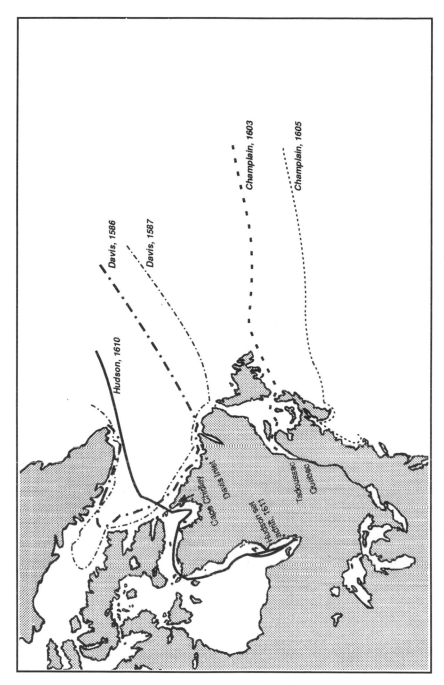

"Perfect hope of a Passage:" explorers in search of a route through, or around, North America and on to the "blessed shores of Cathay."

As England's sea power increased, her relations with Spain deteriorated. This was, in no small part, because of the crown-sanctioned privateering of the likes of Hawkins and Drake, who were treated as heroes in their native country. English relations with the Portuguese had been much friendlier, being based on trade and upon their respective dealings in the New-Founde-Land, where the English were accustomed to rely on the Portuguese for salt. But, in 1578 the Portuguese King Sebastien, died in battle with the Moors. Thereafter, the Portuguese crown was allied with that of Spain, so that during the 1580s, Portuguese vessels also came to be regarded by the English as fair game for privateers and the Portuguese fishery began to decline.

There were many advocates of increased English exploration and colonization in the New World. One of the most enthusiastic was Richard Hakluyt the younger, a clergyman, and lecturer at Oxford University. In 1582, Hakluyt published his first book, *Divers voyages touching the discoverie of America*, in which he collected documents concerning early voyages, in addition to unearthing such cogent items as John Cabot's letters patent of 1496. By this time, the Cabot "discoverie" had been all but forgotten, and with it England's claim to Newfoundland. Hakluyt emphasized England's responsibility to assert her naval power over the French and Spanish, and to claim possession of new lands. In addition to recognizing the strategic importance of the New-Founde-Land station, Hakluyt also supported the efforts of those such as Humphrey Gilbert and Dr. Dee, who were promoting the potential of a discovery of a new, northern route around America to the Indies — well away from the Spanish and Portuguese colonies. It was Humphrey Gilbert who had given this supposed northern route its popular name, the "NorthWest Passage", in his *Discourse of a discoverie for a new passage to Cataia*. The book was presumed to have been written and circulated in 1566, but not published until ten years later.

Geographical knowledge was being added to year by year — yet the east coast of North America, north of the Strait of Belle Isle was little known. In the early 1500s, both Gaspar Corte Real and Sebastian Cabot had made voyages to the north. Cabot claimed to have reached 67°30'N and found the sea open and navigable, but this has been dismissed by historians as exaggeration. There had been no useful description of the Labrador coast. Some maps of the mid-1500s showed a large bay or river, north of the Strait of Belle Isle — indicating knowledge of Groswater Bay/Hamilton Inlet — but it was more typical for the Land of the Labrador to be dismissed as of little consequence. One map, prepared in 1529, had it in a legend: "this land was discovered by the English, nothing in it of any value". There was equally little knowledge of the existence of Greenland.

After 1558, the situation was considerably confused by the publication of the Zeno map. Later revealed as a hoax, the Zeno map purported to show northern lands discovered by the Venetian brothers Nicolo and Antonio Zeno, in about 1390. The Zeno map showed fairly convincing representations of Iceland and Greenland to the northwest of Britain. It also showed a large island to the south of Greenland ("Frisland") and two lands to the west: Estotiland and Drogeo — which armchair geographers were quick to identify with Labrador and Newfoundland. Most significantly, the false Zeno map showed a large strait between Estotiland/Labrador and Greenland, with a further expanse of open sea to the north and west. It was this false sea that attracted the attention of Gilbert in his *Discourse*, and provided the impetus for the first English voyage of discovery to the North West Passage, that of Martin Frobisher, in 1576.

Frobisher rounded the southern tip of Greenland and, after encountering ice, sailed to the west into "Frobisher's Streights", which he believed to separate the "Horn of Asia" in the north, from America to the south. Now known as Frobisher Bay, this was actually an inlet on Baffin Island. He returned to England optimistic that he had proven the Passage. Frobisher also brought back some black stone "in token of Christian possession", which was soon mistakenly pronounced to be rich gold ore. This led to the formation of the Company of Cathay (with the Queen herself investing 1000 pounds) and two further voyages by Frobisher, in 1577 and 1578. The search for the Passage was put aside in the false hope of establishing profitable mines.

Frobisher's misunderstandings about northern geography, partly caused by trying to fit his discoveries into the Zeno model, led him to believe not only that he had discovered the Passage, but also that he had reached Frisland, although, not surprisingly, he was unable to land. The Frobisher voyages also added their own element of confusion, in that the explorer claimed to have seen another previously unknown island, which he placed southeast of Frisland — the Land of Buss. Although Davis later visited Frobisher Bay, he did not recognize it as being ''Frobisher's Streights''. He considered Frobisher to have discovered a genuine strait, through southern Greenland.

In 1583, Sir Humphrey Gilbert formally took possession of the New-Founde-Land for England. This was in the course of a colonization venture to Virginia that was later aborted. On the return journey, he, and all on his ship, disappeared beneath the waves in a savage storm. A chronicler of Gilbert's journey watched from another ship and recorded the tragic event. Yet the loss of Gilbert — and his last words: ''we are as neare to Heaven by sea as by land'' — led to his *Discourse* taking on something of a heroic call to duty to his younger brother Adrian, as well as to Adrian Gilbert's friend, John Davis. (Davis christened his first child, born that year, Gilbert.) Adrian Gilbert was soon drawn into the confidence of John Dee. Dee had, in 1580, been assigned the portion of Humphrey Gilbert's

An artist's conception of John Dee, Adrian Gilbert, Sir Francis Walsingham, and John Davis discussing the Northwest Passage. (From Clements Markham's *A Life of John Davis*, 1889.)

grant north of 50°N and soon became the leading advocate of the North West Passage.

Early in 1584, Dr. Dee and Adrian Gilbert were engaged in discussion of the nature of the Arctic regions, when they were joined by a most influential person indeed: the Secretary of State, Sir Francis Walsingham. Walsingham's interest was piqued. The next day a further meeting was arranged between Walsingham, Dee, Gilbert and the accomplished and practical mariner — John Davis. Dr. Dee's journal notes of that meeting ''only we four were secret, and we made Mr. Secretary privie of the North-West Passage''. That spring, Dee and Gilbert conferred with persons of political influence, and with members of the London merchant community, attempting to arrange backing for a new voyage of discovery, under the command of Davis.

In the midst of these negotiations, Dr. Dee departed for Europe. His home was subsequently burned to the ground by neighbours who suspected Dee of practising magic. Adrian Gilbert then turned to his half-brother, Sir Walter Raleigh, a favourite of the Queen and one who was much interested in the exploration and colonizing of North America. Raleigh persuaded the Queen to issue a charter ''for the search and discoverie of the North-West Passage to China'' jointly to himself, Adrian Gilbert and Davis. Every bit as important, Raleigh introduced Davis to a wealthy London merchant, William Sanderson, who was married to Raleigh's niece. With Sanderson's deep interest in geography and equally deep pockets, the voyage was now assured of financial as well as political support. They proposed to begin the voyage early the following summer.

The expedition consisted of just two ships: the flagship *Sunneshine* (50 tons, under the command of Davis) and the *Mooneshine* (35 tons). Accompanying Davis on the *Sunneshine* was Sanderson's nephew, John Janes, who shipped as supercargo. Thanks to Janes's account of the voyage, we have a detailed crew list for the flagship: in addition to Davis and Janes, the ship's company consisted of a master and master's mate, a bosun, gunner, carpenter, eleven seamen, four musicians (whose playing was intended to earn the goodwill of the natives) and a boy, Christopher Hughes.

This voyage left Dartmouth on 7 June 1585. They explored some distance north along the west coast of Greenland, which Davis named the "Land of Desolation", later writing that "the irksome noise of the ice and the loathsome view of the shore bred strange conceits among us". The expedition next sailed west to Baffin Island, across what is now Davis Strait, and explored Cumberland Sound on the east coast of Baffin, in hopes that it might prove to be a passage.

Arriving back in Dartmouth on 30 September, Davis learned of events that had taken place during his absence, that were to have a bearing on England's relationship with Spain. Relations had been deteriorating for some time, and just before Davis's departure, the Spanish had declared an embargo on English shipping, blockading several vessels in the northern Spanish port of Bilbao. It was decided to release a number of privateers to harass the Spanish in retaliation. On 10 June (just three days after the *Sunneshine* had sailed), Raleigh was authorized to impress ships to warn the New-Founde-Land fishing fleet. Among the captains dispatched were Bernard Drake and Davis's brother-in-law, Andrew Fulford, who had both been originally engaged as part of a expedition to Raleigh's newly-established colony on Roanoke Island in North Carolina. The English captured more than 20 Portuguese fishing vessels, a blow which effectively ended the Portuguese presence in Terra Nova. On being brought back to Devon, the Portuguese brought back a "great sickness" (presumed to be typhus), and an epidemic raged in the West Country for the next year. Among the early victims of the sickness were a number of judges, justices of the peace and jurors at the port of Exeter — who had convened to question the Portuguese, concerning reports that they had been mistreated by their captors. Andrew Fulford succumbed to this "great sickness". His widow subsequently married Adrian Gilbert.

Meantime, Davis had reported to Sir Francis Walsingham, "the North-West Passage is a matter nothing doubtful, but at any tyme almost to be passed, the sea navigable, voyd of yse, the ayre tolerable, and the waters very depe". Two voyages later, the existence of the North West Passage still remained unknown. Davis wrote optimistically to Sanderson on 16 September 1587: "The passage is most probable, the execution easie". Yet, while Davis's later two voyages did not find the passage, they did make notable contributions to geographic knowledge of that extensive coastline, that which we now know as Labrador.

On his second voyage, Davis made an earlier start, leaving Dartmouth on 7 May, with his two original ships, plus a larger vessel, the *Mermayde* (120 tons), and a pinnace of 10 tons, the *North Star*. The *Sunneshine* and *North Star* were dispatched to search north along the east coast of Greenland, where the pinnace was lost with all hands. The others continued to Davis Strait. Proving unwieldy in ice, the *Mermayde* was returned to England and Davis continued exploring Greenland in the *Mooneshine*. He was eventually stopped by ice, then again coasted Baffin Island in search of a passage, continuing south along the Labrador coast. Davis's own account of the voyage along Labrador follows:

> *We coasted this land till the eight and twentieth of August, finding it still to continue towards the south from the latitude of 67 to 57 degrees. We found marvellous great store of birds, gulls and mews, incredible to be reported [probably off Fish Island, north of Nain]; whereupon, being calm weather, we lay one glass upon the lee to prove for fish, in which space we caught 100 cod, although we were but badly provided for fishing, not being our purpose. This eight and twentieth, having great distrust of the weather, we arrived in a very fair harbour in the latitude of 56 degrees [near what is now Davis Inlet], and sailed 10 leagues into the same, being two leagues broad, with very fair woods on both sides. In this place we continued until the first of September, in which time we had two very great storms. I landed, and went six miles by guess into the country, and found that the woods were fir, pineapple, alder, yew, withy, and birch. Here we saw a black bear. This place yieldeth great store of birds, as pheasant, partridge, Barbary hen of the like, wild geese, duck, blackbirds, jays, thrushes, with other kinds of small birds. Of the partridge and pheasant we killed great store with bow and arrows. In this place at the harbour mouth we found great store of cod".*
>
> *The first of September at ten o'clock we set sail and coasted the shore with very fair weather. The third day being calm, at noon we struck sail and let fall a kedge anchor, to prove*

A Newfoundland fishing ship of the 1600s, from a map cartouche of 1710.
(Courtesy Parks Canada.)

whether we could take any fish, being in latitude 54 degrees 30 minutes, in which place we found great abundance of cod so that the hook was no sooner overboard but presently a fish was taken [on the north side of Groswater Bay, possibly off Brig Harbour Island or White Cockade]. It was the largest and the best-fed fish that ever I saw, and divers fishermen that were with me said that they never saw a more suaule [suitable?] or better school of fish in their lives, yet had they seen great abundance.

The fourth of September at five o'clock in the afternoon we anchored in a very good road among great store of isles, the country low land, pleasant, and very full of fair woods [Trunmore Bay, just south of Cape Porcupine]. To the north of this place eight leagues we had a perfect hope of the passage, finding a mighty great sea passing between two lands west [probably The Narrows, the entrance to Lake Melville, near Rigolet]. The south land to our judgment being nothing but isles, we greatly desired to go into this sea but the wind was directly against us. We anchored in four fathom fine sand. In this place is fowl and fish mighty store.

The sixth of September, having a fair north-north-west wind, having trimmed our bark we purposed to depart, and sent five of our sailors, young men, ashore to an island to fetch certain fish which we purposed to weather and therefore left it all night covered upon the isle. The brutish people of this country lay secretly lurking in the wood, and upon the sudden assaulted our men; which when we perceived we presently let slip our cables upon the hawse and under our foresail bore into the shore, and with all expedition discharged a double musket upon them twice, at the noise whereof they fled. Notwithstanding, to our very great grief, two of our men were slain with their arrows and two grievously wounded, of whom at this present we stand in very great doubt. Only one escaped by swimming, with an arrow shot through his arm. These wicked miscreants never offered parley or speech, but presently executed their cursed fury.

This present evening it pleased God further to increase our sorrows with a mighty tempestuous storm, the wind being north-north-east, which lasted unto the tenth of this month very extreme. We unrigged our ship, and proposed to cut down our masts, the cable of our sheet-anchor broke, so that we only expected to be driven on shore among these cannibals for their prey. Yet in this deep distress the mighty mercy of God, when hope was past, gave us succour, and sent us a fair lee so as we recovered our anchor again and new-moored our ship; where we saw that God manifestly delivered us, for the strands of one of old cables were broken and we only rode by an old junk [that is, an old rope]. Thus being freshly moored, a new storm arose, the wind being west-north-west, very forcible, which lasted unto the tenth day at night.

The eleventh day with a fair west-north-west wind we departed with trust in God's mercy, shaping our course for England, and arrived in the west country in the beginning of October. [23]

Given that accounts of the Davis voyages provide some of the most sympathetic and detailed early accounts of the Inuit in the Canadian Arctic, it is unfortunate that the only extended encounter that Davis had with the natives of the Labrador coast, just north of Sandwich Bay, was so unfavourable. There is little in the account of the ''wicked miscreants'' to identify them as Innu.

Davis returned, still convinced that the passage was within his grasp. Rather than assuming a strait between America and the mythical Horn of Asia, his assessment was now that ''the north parts of America are all islands'' and that, in all the immense coastline he had laid down for the first time, the "Passage is in one of four places, or not at all''. His backers in Exeter had by this time lost enthusiasm, as Davis later noted, ''all the westerne marchant-adventurers fell from the action''.

Once again the most significant discovery, despite all talk of a passage to China, would appear to have been fishing grounds, initially discovered by observing the numbers of seabirds off the Labrador coast north of Nain:

...having divers fishermen aboord our barke, they all concluded that there was a great skull of fish; we, being unprovided of fishing furniture, with a long spike nayle made a hooke and fastened the same to one of our sounding lines. Before the baite was changed we took more than fortie great cods, the fish swimming so abundantly thicke about our barke as is incredible to bee reported. ... [24]

---

23   Hakluyt, Richard. *The Principal Navigations ... of the English Nation.* Vol. VII. New York: AMS Press Inc., 1965. p.405-407.

With the enthusiasm of his backers waning, Davis hit upon a plan to support a third voyage in 1587. He proposed that the unprofitable business of exploration should be subsidized by bringing along two vessels to engage in the fishery (the *Sunneshine* and the *Elizabeth*), while Davis conducted the actual exploration from a clinker-built pinnace, the *Ellen*, a vessel of only 20 tons. The vessels left Dartmouth on 19 May and one month later were off the coast of Greenland. Having only been persuaded to accompany the explorer this far ''after much talk and many threatenings'', the two fishing vessels made for Groswater Bay, where Davis intended to meet with them later. As it took only 16 days to load both vessels at this virgin fishing ground, they returned to England without making the rendezvous — or indeed erecting the agreed-upon signs, perhaps suggesting that, with the promise of the profits from the fishery, they were prepared to give up the *Ellen* for lost.

After the party split up, Davis sailed the tiny *Ellen* north along what he named the ''London Coast'' of Greenland, eventually reaching 72°12'N (near present-day Upernavik). Although forced to turn back by northerly winds, he noted that the sea ahead appeared ice-free. This vast polynya (or naturally-occurring open patch in the pack ice) later became known to whalers as the North Water — and Davis's account of it was the origin of the myth of an open Polar Sea to the north of the pack ice. Turning south, Davis found his way to the west blocked by the Middle Pack of ice in Baffin Bay. He eventually reached the coast of Baffin Island, satisfied himself that Cumberland Sound was no passage and bypassed Frobisher Bay (which he named ''Lord Lumley's Inlet''). South of Frobisher Bay, he noted a ''furious overfall'' or meeting of the tides, which we now know as the opening of Hudson Strait:

> *We fell into a mighty rase, where an island of ice was carried*
> *by the force of current as fast as our barke could sail ... we*
> *saw the sea falling down into the gulfe with a mighty overfal,*
> *and roring, with divers circular motions like whirlepooles, in*

---

24   Hakluyt, Richard. *The Principal Navigations ... of the English Nation.*
       Vol.VII. New York: AMS Press Inc., 1965. p.443.

such sort as forcible streams passe thorow the arches of
bridges.... [25]

Prevented from entering the Strait by ice and current, Davis
proceeded south, naming the southern headland after a Devonshire
captain (Cape Chidley, the northernmost point of Labrador). The rest of
the voyage down the Labrador coast is described by Janes, who once
again accompanied the voyage to protect the interests of Sanderson.

> *The first of August, having coasted a bank of ice which was*
> *driven out at the mouth of this gulf, we fell with the southermost*
> *cape of the gulf, which we named Chidley's Cape, which lay in*
> *61 degrees and 10 minutes of latitude. The 2nd and 3rd were*
> *calm and foggy; so were the 4th, 5th, and 6th. The 7th was fair*
> *and calm, so was the 8th, with a little gale in the morning. The*
> *9th was fair, and we had a little gale at night. The 10th we had*
> *a frisking gale at west-north-west, the 11th fair. The 12th we*
> *saw five deer [caribou] on the top of an island, called by us*
> *Darcy's Island; and we hoisted out our boat and went ashore to*
> *them, thinking to have killed some of them. But when we came*
> *on shore and had coursed them twice about the island, they took*
> *the sea and swam towards islands distant from us the three*
> *leagues. When we perceived that they had taken the sea we*
> *gave them over, because our boat was so small that it could not*
> *carry us and row after them, they swam so fast; but one of them*
> *was big as a good pretty cow, and very fat, their feet as big as*
> *ox feet. Here upon this island I killed with my piece a grey hare.*
>
> *The 13th in the morning we saw three or four white bears,*
> *but durst not go on shore to them for lack of good boat. This*
> *day we struck a rock, seeking for a harbour, and received a*
> *leak; and this day we were in 54 degrees of latitude [the south*
> *side of Groswater Bay]. The 14th we stopped our leak, in a*
> *storm not very outrageous, at noon.*

---

25   Hakluyt, Richard. *The Principal Navigations ... of the English Nation.*
     Vol.VII. New York: AMS Press Inc., 1965. p.435.

The 15th, being almost in 52 degrees of latitude [that is, nearing the entrance to the Strait of Belle Isle] and not finding our ships, nor (according to their promise) any kind of mark, token, of beacon, which we willed them to set up, and they protested to do so, upon every headland, island, or cape within twenty leagues every way off from their fishing place, which our Captain appointed to be between 54 and 55 degrees: this 15th, I say, we shaped our course homeward. ...

The 17th we met a ship at sea, and as far as we could judge it was a Biscayan [Spanish Basque]. We thought she went a-fishing for whales, for in 52 degrees or thereabout we saw very many. The 18th was fair, with a good gale at west; the 19th fair also, with much wind at west and by south. And thus after much variable weather and change of winds we arrived the 15th of September in Dartmouth anno 1587, giving thanks to God for our safe arrival. [26]

Davis returned to find that relations with Spain had worsened further, and that an invasion of England was threatened. With the death of Walsingham soon afterward, "the voyage was friendless", and additional exploration was put on hold. Davis spent the next three years in naval service connected with the Spanish War. As master of the *Black Dog*, tender to the Lord Admiral's *Ark Royal*, Davis played a small role in the defeat of the Spanish Armada in 1588 and later harassed Spanish shipping to good effect. The great victory over Spain resulted in a much diminished Spanish navy and altered the nature of the Newfoundland fishery. The French continued to dominate the northern fishery. The Spanish and Portuguese dropped out, and the English fishery greatly increased.

With the war's end, in 1591 Davis again joined a voyage of exploration, this time a circumnavigation of the globe led by Thomas Cavendish. Davis's intention was that once the expedition had cleared the Straits of Magellan into the Pacific Ocean, he should sail

---

26 Hakluyt, Richard. *The Principal Navigations ... of the English Nation.* Vol. VII. New York: AMS Press Inc., 1965. p.421-422.

north along the "backe side of America" and seek out a western entrance to the passage. However, this voyage was a disastrous failure, ending in the deaths of Cavendish and all but 15 of Davis's crew of 76 from shipwreck or from scurvy. Davis limped back to England in command of the remnants of the expedition, his only real achievement being the discovery of the Falkland Islands.

Davis was in poor health for the next few years. He also endured a personal trial in finding that during his absence his wife had been "seduced", thus ending his marriage: Davis turned to writing. In 1594, he brought out the first edition of his *Seamen's secrets*, the first navigation and seamanship manual produced specifically for the needs of English seamen. The next year, he published a book that attempted to again rally support for the search of a North West Passage, *"The worldes hydrographic discription, wherein it is proved ... that the World in all his zones climates and places is habitable, and the sea likewise universally navigable ... whereby it appears that from England there is a short and spedie passage to India by northerly navigation"*.

Davis's writings constituted an important addition to the knowledge of both geography and practical navigation. In *The worldes hydrographic discription*, he related the experiments he had performed on ice bergs and pack ice during his northern voyages. He supplied for the first time, an account of how icebergs were formed by calving from Greenland glaciers, as well as discussions of the flotation of sea ice and how bergs "founder" at sea. There were also careful observations on the terrain, rock formations, weather, flora, fauna and native peoples of Greenland, Baffin Island and Labrador. His *Seamen's secrets* contained valuable information concerning compass variation in the north, a state-of-the-art treatise on the problems of determining longitude, and reproduced pages from the "Traverse Book"(ships log) of Davis's 1587 voyage on the *Ellen*. The Davis "Traverse Book" was adopted as the English standard for a ship's log.

Davis returned to exploration in 1598 when he was appointed pilot to the second Dutch expedition to the East Indies. This voyage lasted until 1600. On his return, he was appointed chief pilot to the newly-formed English "East India Company" and made a further voyage, which lasted until 1603. Next, Davis was pilot to an Indies

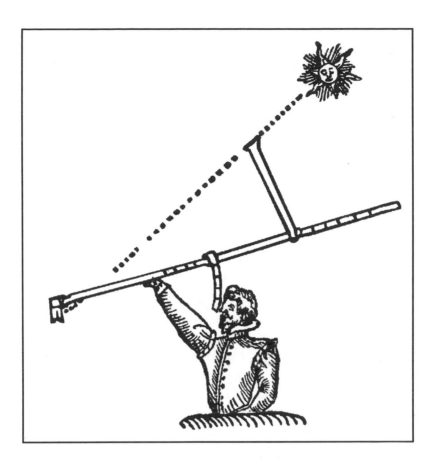

The back staff, from *Seamen's Secrets.*

The single greatest advance in seamanship attributed to Davis was his invention for determining latitude, by observation of the sun. Of all his inventions, this was the most simple and most useful to mariners. Davis originally called his invention a "backstaff", as it performed the same function as the earlier crosstaff, but without the necessity of sighting into the glare of the sun. As he explained in Seamen's Secrets, the observer directed a slit in the plate at the end of the staff at the horizon, then slid the top arm along the scale on the staff until its shadow "doe fall directly upon the said slitte", measuring the height on the scale. During his period of "retirement" after the Cavendish expedition, the explorer refined this invention into the "Davis Quadrant" — an invention that was not improved upon as a means of determining latitude until nearly 150 years later, in 1731.

expedition led by Sir Edward Michelborne. Late in 1605, Michelborne took a Japanese pirate ship in custody off the east coast of Malaya. During a search of their ship, the pirates broke loose, killing Davis as their first victim.

John Davis was the first North American explorer to take both a scholarly and eminently practical approach to the problems of seamanship. Davis was highly regarded by both his crews and his naval colleagues. His North American explorations, in particular, also made a significant contribution to the geographic knowledge of his time. His particular concern with the problem of the North West Passage and his useful summary of what was known about this region in *The worldes hydrographic discription* led to further voyages in search of the passage in the early 1600s, the best known of which is Henry Hudson's voyage of 1610.

In terms of geographical knowledge of Labrador, Davis's were the first descriptions of that coast north of the Strait of Belle Isle, while his accounts of the ''great store of cod'' there, may be taken as the beginning point of the Labrador fishery. While Davis was unable to return to the scene of his labours due to a lack of sponsorship, he had hit upon one unique scheme: that of supporting exploration by the fishery. In the years that followed, further expansion of geographic knowledge was to be tied up with the expanding fishery and attempts to make a profit from the New-Founde-Land.

Samuel de Champlain is best known to history as the founder of the Quebec colony and an explorer of the Canadian hinterland. "The Father of New France" made numerous voyages as well as overland explorations during the period 1603 to 1615 — along the New England coast, the Bay of Fundy, the Ottawa River, and into the Great Lakes by ship, on foot, and by birchback canoe.

There is no evidence that Champlain ever actually set foot upon the New-Founde-Land. Yet, he was the son of a sea captain of Brouage, had extensive contacts in Honfleur and St. Malo, made 21 Atlantic crossings, and was extremely well-acquainted with New-Founde-Land waters. From the journal of his first voyage to the ''river of Canada'' (the St. Lawrence), in 1603:

We came upon the Bank in lat 44°20'. On the 6th so near the land we heard the sea beat on the shore but could not see it for the thickness of the fog, to which these coasts are subject; and on this account we again put out to sea some leagues, until the next morning, when the weather being very clear, we sighted land, which was Cape St. Mary's.

The next day, the twelfth, we were overtaken by a great gale of wind, which lasted two days. On the fifteenth of the same month we sighted the islands of St. Pierre. On the 17th we met with an ice-floe near Cape Ray, six leagues in length, which caused us to strike sail the whole night...

On this voyage, Champlain's ship, on departing Honfleur, made for New-Founde-Land waters en route to the St. Lawrence — much as Jacques Cartier had done. Like Cartier, Champlain was searching for a way through the continental land mass, to the "blessed shores of Cathay." It was only after Champlain had, with his own eyes, determined that there was no new route to be found to the east, that he threw himself into the role for which he best known, as the founder of the Quebec colony.

Champlain first came to North America as a geographer, accompanying a small fur-trading expedition. He made the voyage which resulted in the founding of Quebec in 1608. Later in his career, he produced several maps of eastern North America, which reflected both the state of the art in map making and his first-hand knowledge of the coast. His contribution to North American cartography lies largely in the detail he added from his travels, in what are now the Maritime Provinces, and on to the Great Lakes. Champlain's larger charts incorporated up-to-date maps of the New-Founde-Land and the adjoining fishing banks.

The career of Samuel de Champlain spans the close of the Age of Discovery and the opening of an era of settlement. From 1604 to 1607, he was involved in attempts to settle in the Bay of Fundy, and, the following year used the lessons learned to found the first permanent garrison and "habitation" at Quebec, where he remained in command until his death in 1635.

Like Davis and Champlain, Henry Hudson began his explorations of the New World with "perfect hope of a Passage". Like Champlain, Hudson opened up a previously-unknown route into the North American interior. Indeed, the two explorers very nearly met in the late summer of 1609. As Hudson began his ascent of what is now the Hudson River in the state of New York, Champlain was returning to Quebec from a battle he had fought with the Iroquois just a few miles away, at what is now Crown Point, N.Y.

Hudson's reputation as an explorer had been made while in the employ of the Muscovy Company — which was still expanding their profitable Russian trade, a half-century after the Company had been founded by Sebastian Cabot. In 1609 the Dutch East India Company hired Hudson, with a mixed crew of Dutch and English, to continue the search for a Northeast Passage, around northern Asia. His crew mutinied when faced with the northern ice. Hudson re-directed the voyage to "China" — and so, as mate Robert Juet wrote, they "steered away west for *Newfound Land*". They explored the eastern seaboard of North America before ascending the river which now bears Hudson's name and reaching a dead-end, near what is now Albany, New York. On his return to England, Hudson found that the English Privy Council had issued an order forbidding him from returning to the Netherlands.

The next year, Hudson and an English crew set out on a dramatic voyage, via Iceland and Greenland, to Davis Strait, searching for a Northwest Passage in the vicinity of the "furious overfall" noted by John Davis off Cape Chidley. A mutiny was barely brought under control as the 55-ton *Discovery* attempted to navigate the ice-strewn tide-race, now known as Hudson Strait. Early in August they arrived at the "spacious sea" which would also take the explorer's name. Hudson turned south, convinced that he had "won the passage." But that fall found the *Discovery* anchored at the mouth of the Rupert River in James Bay, and by November 10th, the ship and crew were frozen in. They were not able to extricate their ship until June 12, 1611 — by which time hunger was a pressing problem. Hudson, having noted "mighty tides" to the northwest, was seemingly determined to continue the search for an outlet into the Pacific. Added to festering disputes between the crew and Hudson, and a rumour that the captain was hoarding food, the captain's single-minded disregard for his starving crew led to a mutiny. On

June 23rd. Hudson and eight crewmen were set adrift in Hudson Bay, and were never heard from again.

Three of the mutineers were later killed by natives and one died of starvation. In the fall of 1611 the *Discovery* sailed south along the Labrador coast and the crew debated whether to make for New-Founde-Land, where it was presumed the fishers might have left behind dried fish or other food. The account left by Abacuck Prickett, supercargo of the *Discovery*, noted that the crew voted to ''seek food where wee knew corne grew, and not where it was cast away, and not to bee founde'' and so made for England. Only eight of twenty-one survived the voyage.

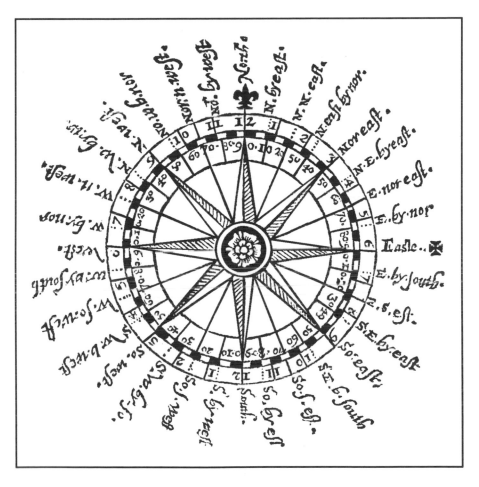

Compass card, from John Davis' *Seamen's Secrets.*

Ironically, the very summer that the *Discovery* had entered Hudson Bay, John Guy had led a group of Bristol colonists who over-wintered in the New-Founde-Land at Cuper's Cove (Cupids), Conception Bay. After that first winter, Guy had reported on the success of their crops. "Such was the state of things with us as we were in no want of victuals, but had a great remainder". Of course, the crew of the *Discovery* had no knowledge of the existence of the Cuper's Cove colony.

John Davis had provided the first written description of the coasts north of the Strait of Belle Isle, and so "lighted Hudson into his streights." Davis had also hit upon a unique scheme: supporting exploration by fishing. In the years that followed, as European nations built upon the pioneer colonies founded by the likes of Samuel de Champlain and John Guy, further exploration was done by adventurers who wished to exploit the land and sea resources of the New World, or were themselves settlers in the New-Founde-Lands.

9.

The Native Peoples.

The burial mound at L'Anse Amour.

Archaeologists at work on a Recent Indian/Beothuk site at Dildo Pond.
(Courtesy William Gilbert.)

L eaving aside the questions surrounding Irish monks, Norse settlers, and the competing Cabot "landfalls," there is less controversy in stating that what is now the Province of Newfoundland and Labrador was almost certainly discovered by the earliest inhabitants of southern Labrador. Known to archaeologists as Palaeo-Indians, these people occupied coastal sites on the Labrador side of the Strait of Belle Isle about 9000 years ago. Although there is no physical evidence of any inhabitation of the Island itself over the following 4000 years, these people might also be regarded as the "discoverers" of Newfoundland. The tip of the Great Northern Peninsula is visible from the Labrador side of the Strait, which is merely nine miles wide at its narrowest point. The peninsula could have even been visited on occasion, although no archaeological evidence supports this conjecture.

From the first, the human cultures in Newfoundland and Labrador have been nourished and defined by the resources of the sea. The Strait of Belle Isle was of great importance to prehistoric inhabitants because it was extremely rich in marine life. In the Strait, cold arctic waters from a branch of the Labrador current, meet the warmer, nutrient-rich waters of the Gulf of St. Lawrence, providing a perfect environment for the growth of plankton. These microscopic plants and animals are the lowest link in the marine food chain, making the Strait a rich ground for fish and seabirds as well.

The tidal currents through the Strait were also important in making this area hospitable to prehistoric peoples, because these currents usually prevent the formation of solid sea-ice for most of the winter. This fact, along with the richness of plankton, makes the Strait a favourable environment for marine mammals, such as whales and particularly seals. Similarly, the narrow Strait also makes it comparatively easy for people to hunt seals from shore.

This separation of the Province at the Strait of Belle Isle is also one of great geological significance. Labrador forms the easternmost part of the Canadian Shield, a vast geological region that contains some of the oldest rocks on earth. The rocks of the Canadian Shield have been almost unaffected by what geologists call "tectonic events" (better known to the rest of us as "continental drift"). Much of the Island of Newfoundland, however, is the northeasternmost extension of the Appalachian system, which forms the eastern

The Maritime Archaic expand to northern Labrador.	**3000** BC	*The Great Pyramid of Giza is built in Egypt.*
The earliest evidence of Maritime Archaic inhabitation of the Island of Newfoundland, on the Great Northern Peninsula and the northeast coast.		
Intensive Maritime Archaic use of Port au Choix.	**2000** BC	
Palaeo-Eskimo people migrate from the Arctic islands to northern Labrador.		
The extinction or retreat of the Maritime Archaic.	**1500** BC	*The "Bronze Age" begins in Europe.*
	1300 BC	*The Exodus of the Hebrews.*
The apparent disappearance of the Maritime Archaic culture.	**1000** BC	*The Phoenicians begin their expansion/trade in the eastern Mediterranean.*
Early Dorset Eskimo begin their expansion into southern Labrador.		
	800 BC	*Homer's Iliad.*
	750 BC	*The Greek city-states begin their expansion.*
	600 BC	*Reputed circumnavigation of Africa by Phoenicians.*
	500 BC	*Transition to the Iron Age in Europe.* *Death of Confucius.*
	334 BC	*Alexander the Great invades Asia Minor*

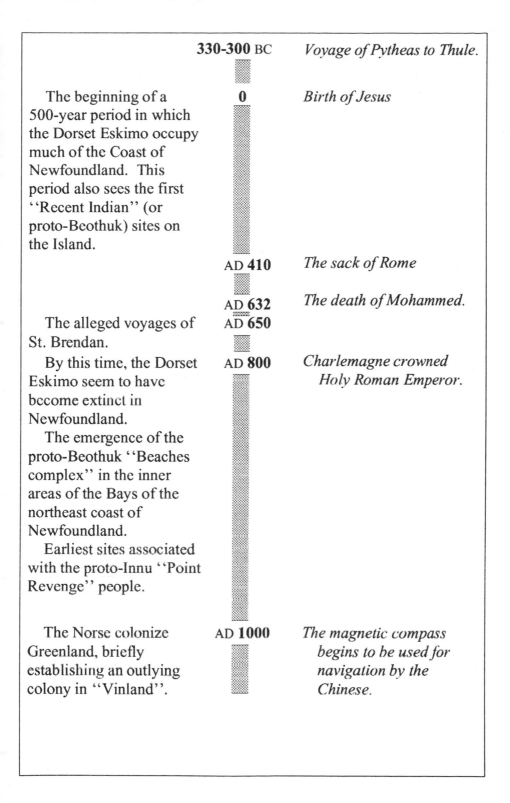

	330-300 BC	*Voyage of Pytheas to Thule.*
The beginning of a 500-year period in which the Dorset Eskimo occupy much of the Coast of Newfoundland. This period also sees the first "Recent Indian" (or proto-Beothuk) sites on the Island.	**0**	*Birth of Jesus*
	AD **410**	*The sack of Rome*
	AD **632**	*The death of Mohammed.*
The alleged voyages of St. Brendan.	AD **650**	
By this time, the Dorset Eskimo seem to have become extinct in Newfoundland.	AD **800**	*Charlemagne crowned Holy Roman Emperor.*
The emergence of the proto-Beothuk "Beaches complex" in the inner areas of the Bays of the northeast coast of Newfoundland.		
Earliest sites associated with the proto-Innu "Point Revenge" people.		
The Norse colonize Greenland, briefly establishing an outlying colony in "Vinland".	AD **1000**	*The magnetic compass begins to be used for navigation by the Chinese.*

seaboard of North America, extending all the way south into the state of Georgia. Geologists have demonstrated that the Island was formed through drift and collision — a series of geological events that have been dubbed ''the Harry Hibbs effect'', after a well-known Newfoundland accordion player.

The other major factor affecting the landforms of Newfoundland and Labrador has been extensive glaciation, during a series of prehistoric events commonly known as ''Ice Ages''. The most recent Ice Age, the Wisconsin Glaciation, lasted from about 100,000 to 15,000 years ago — followed by a period of glacial retreat, lasting perhaps 5,000 years. The ''Late Wisconsin Glaciation'' reached its maximum extent from about 20,000 to 15,000 years ago. During the Late Wisconsin, most of central and northern Labrador were covered by the Laurentide ice sheet, a massive dome of ice centred over Hudson Bay and northeastern Quebec. The southern Labrador coast and portions of the north coast were probably ice-free. In contrast to the massive glacier covering much of Labrador, the Island was glaciated in the Late Wisconsin by several much smaller ice domes, the largest of which were over the central part, along the axis of the Long Range Mountains of the west coast, and over the Avalon Peninsula.

Particularly in Labrador, because of the massive Laurentide ice dome, the weight of the glaciers caused the earth's crust to be pressed down and, in coastal areas, submerged. The retreat of the glaciers, caused a ''re-emergence'' of the coastline. When the Strait of Belle Isle was first settled, the coastline was re-emerging from the sea at a rate of about four metres every 100 years. Thus, the original inhabitants lived along a coastline that was inland from that of present-day southern Labrador. One result of this re-emergence is that archaeologists can estimate roughly the age of ''coastal'' campsites from their height above sea level. The site generally considered to contain the oldest evidence of human habitation in the province is located near Pinware, Labrador, about 27 metres above sea level. Both land and sea were rising during this period. But while the land in southern Labrador rose at a much faster rate than the increase in sea level, elsewhere in the Atlantic Provinces, the rate of the rise of the sea due to glacial meltwater was faster than the rate of re-emergence of the land. Consequently, many ancient coastal sites that might show a more complete picture of prehistoric human life in the region have become submerged.

By 10,000 BC, Palaeo-Indians occupied much of central and southern North America. The northern group of this big-game-hunting people spread further to the north and hunted in the tundra-like conditions of the glacial fringe. As the climate warmed and forests grew, many large herd animals (including mammoths, giant bison, horses and camels) died out. Probably this resulted from a combination of ecological changes and intensive hunting by Palaeo-Indians. Thus, Palaeo-Indian culture began to fragment as different groups spread out and adapted to changing local conditions and resources.

There is archaeological evidence of Palaeo-Indian habitation in the Maritime Provinces by about 9000 BC, but it was probably another 1000 years before these people crossed the St. Lawrence River and began to make their way north toward Labrador. (Because sea levels along the St. Lawrence estuary have risen since prehistoric times, intermediate sites that might help date and confirm this conjectured migration were "drowned".)

The earliest inhabitants of Labrador are known from their small "coastal" campsites, unearthed in the mid-1970s, along the Strait of Belle Isle, and dating back to about 7000 BC. Like other Palaeo-Indians in the Maritimes, they were mainly caribou hunters, who probably learned more about the hunting of marine resources as they became established north of the St. Lawrence. By about 5500 BC, there is archaeological evidence that these people were becoming increasingly adapted to a maritime way of life, their distinctive maritime culture known as the Maritime Archaic Tradition.

The abundant resources of the Strait of Belle Isle region caused the big-game-hunting Palaeo-Indian culture to develop into one adapted to coastal life. New styles of tools were developed: barbed bone and stone spear points and — of great importance archaeologically — a "toggling" harpoon. This last tool enters like a harpoon, but the curved head is fastened in the middle, and when the harpoon line is pulled, the head turns across and prevents dislodgement. It is considered a relatively sophisticated device for hunting seals and whales. The world's oldest known specimen of such a toggling harpoon is from a burial mound at L'Anse Amour, Labrador, dated at approximately 5500 BC.

In about 4000 BC, Maritime Archaic peoples began a slow expansion northward, although the Strait of Belle Isle area probably continued to be their "heartland". By 3000 BC, they had spread to northern Labrador, in the process discovering at Ramah Bay, a distinctive deposit of "chert", a flint-like quartz, which could be shaped into hard, sharp pieces, and which soon became the preferred material for making weapon points. Chert probably had spiritual significance as well. It soon began to be traded to the south. Projectile points made from Ramah chert have been found as far south as Maine.

A date of 3000 BC has also been attached to the earliest known human artifacts from the Island of Newfoundland: Maritime Archaic sites have been investigated at L'Anse aux Meadows and at a site known as The Beaches in Bonavista Bay. However, most Maritime Archaic artifacts on the Island date from about 2000 BC, with the most notable sites being The Beaches and Port au Choix.

Meanwhile, the Maritime Archaic in northern Labrador encountered a new people. Known to archaeologists as Palaeo-Eskimos, this new people came to the Canadian Arctic from the west. They were the last wave of prehistoric people to migrate to North America from Siberia. Physically resembling the modern-day Inuit, they presumably spoke a language different from that of the Maritime Archaic and were culturally different as well. The first meeting between the two must have been a dramatic one, as neither had seen other peoples before. Over the next 500 years, it appears that both groups occupied the Labrador coast, with the Palaeo-Eskimos gradually moving south to the area around Nain, while Maritime Archaic continued to occupy sites in the Saglek-Hebron region (controlling access to the Ramah chert) and the Strait of Belle Isle.

This same period saw some interesting developments among the northern branch of the Maritime Archaic; particularly, the emergence of large "longhouse" settlements. These might be attributed to the development of a more hierarchical society, with local "chiefs" becoming boat captains, traders in chert and territorial defenders.

Burials also became more elaborate and it has been suggested that this period of ''first contact'' led to an increase in religious practices. There may also have been friendly relations, including cultural exchanges, between the two. Of particular note is the adaption by Palaeo-Eskimos of the toggling harpoon and the fact that the Maritime Archaic appear to have learned the use of the bow and arrow from the Palaeo-Eskimos. Some archaeologists have speculated that the subsequent spread of the bow and arrow to the Indians of North America occurred as a result of this contact in northern Labrador.

After about 1500 BC, the distinctive stone tools, weapons and burial sites that define the Maritime Archaic cultural tradition disappear from Labrador's archaeological record, while a ''southern branch'' continued on the Island for about another 500 years. While one can speculate that Palaeo-Eskimo expansion was at least partly responsible for the disappearance of the Maritime Archaic in Labrador, there is no indication that such was the case on the Island.

Several possibilities have been suggested to account for this turn of events. A failure of even one of the resources that these people relied on heavily (perhaps seals, caribou, capelin, or salmon) could have made for a precarious existence, while a combined failure of two or more such resources may have made it either impossible to survive or have reduced the population to a point where the remnant becomes ''archaeologically invisible''.

There is a slender thread of evidence that suggests to some archaeologists that descendants from the Maritime Archaic did survive   one small group retreating into the interior around Lake Melville and another to the Strait of Belle Isle. Perhaps one group (or both) became the ancestors of the two Indian groups encountered by the first European visitors: the Beothuk and the Innu.

Meanwhile, what of the Palaeo-Eskimos? As they moved south along the Labrador coast over time, they left fewer sites (at least, fewer that we can now find) suggesting that these people were subject to the same population pressures caused by climactic change or resource scarcity, that appear to have dramatically affected the Maritime Archaic. About 1000 BC, Palaeo-Eskimo sites increase again, perhaps reflecting a new migration into northern Labrador from the Arctic islands. This became known as the "Groswater" phase of Palaeo-Eskimo culture, lasting until about 300 BC. Eventually, Groswater peoples occupied almost the entire coast of Labrador from Saglek to the Strait of Belle Isle, crossing the Strait to occupy all Newfoundland. A notable exception to this occupation is the Avalon Peninsula, which is the most populous area of the Province since the coming of the Europeans.

The late Palaeo-Eskimo (better known as "Dorset") culture first appeared in northern Labrador, and for about the first 500 years AD flourished on the Island as well. Many of the most significant Dorset sites (including The Beaches and Port au Choix) are in areas previously settled by Maritime Archaic. There are comparatively few Dorset sites on the central and southern Labrador coast, where they may have been discouraged by the continuing presence of Indian groups. After about AD 500, the Dorset culture waned on the Island. Yet late Dorset persisted in the Saglek and Nain areas, and small remnant populations may even have continued for nearly 1000 years longer than on the Island, possibly being eventually absorbed by Thule peoples (ancestors of modern-day Inuit), when they reached northern Labrador in about AD 1400.

By about AD 1000, Eskimo groups living in northern Alaska had developed relatively sophisticated methods of hunting large marine mammals (walrus and whales). During a comparatively mild period that lasted from about AD 1000 – 1300, known as the "Medieval Warm", these people, known to archaeologists as the "Thule", invaded Arctic Canada, displacing the communities of the Dorset culture, which were smaller and less advanced technologically. Some legends about this "invasion" have survived in Inuit oral culture, which tell of a docile people known as the "Tunit", who occupied the land before arrival of the Inuit ancestors.

The Thule, who were whale-hunters, spread to the east and north during the Medieval Warm, occupying even the High Arctic islands. After 1250, however, a general cooling of the climate occurred, culminating in about 1600, in what has been called the Little Ice Age. Increased sea-ice probably led both the whales and the Thule to abandon the waters of the High Arctic and they began to depend more on seals, caribou and fish. This coincided with their movement into Labrador and soon in the development of the more mobile culture — the Inuit.

Labrador Inuit and kayak. (Courtesy Harry Cuff Publications.)

The Thule, in addition to having possibly encountered a Dorset remnant, probably also had some contact with ancestral Innu. By AD 1000, an Indian people perhaps descendants of the Maritime Archaic, or a new influx of Indian peoples from the south, again occupied much of the Labrador Peninsula south of Saglek. These "Intermediate Indians" would seem to have adapted to a way of life that involved spending more of the year inland following the caribou, instead of in coastal campsites. As a result, the archaeological record is more obscure.

There is also speculation that a more maritime-oriented recent Indian culture ("Point Revenge") was largely forced by the Thule to abandon hunting and travelling along the coast and became ancestors of the barren-ground Innu (the most northerly branch of this people, previously known as the Naskapi). An alternate theory is that the Intermediate/Point Revenge people became extinct around the time of the European rediscovery of Labrador. If such were the case, then the Innu of Labrador are the descendants of more recent immigrants to Labrador from the Quebec North Shore.

Although it is conceivable that a remnant of the Maritime Archaic people also endured on the Island, it may be more likely that the people who became known as Beothuk descended from the remnant of Maritime Archaic/Intermediate population in southern Labrador, who at some time around AD 500 recolonized the Island. As they tried to wrest a living from their surroundings with fewer large land animals and less dependable sea mammals, few scholars would suggest that the Beothuk of Newfoundland ever numbered as many as 2000, with most estimates ranging between 500 and 1000.

The Beothuk became extinct as a people in 1829. Even though we lived in their midst for 250 years, we know little about them. By far, the majority of documentary accounts concerning this people come from the 1700s, when the northeast coast and Notre Dame Bay were being settled by Europeans. In contrast to settler myths that the Beothuk were a mysterious people of the interior, archaeological research suggests that they were maritime-adapted — spending, in prehistoric times, as many as ten months of the year at coastal campsites, retreating into the country only in fall and early winter, to intercept the annual caribou migrations. Part of the reason the Beothuk had so little contact with European fishermen early in the

Labrador Montagnais (Innu) and trading canoe. (Courtesy Harry Cuff Publications.)

historic period is that the sites favoured by the Beothuk, in the "bottom of the bays", were usually removed from the fishing grounds off the headlands of the bays, the first focus of the European fishery and settlement.

Like most other native peoples, the Beothuk were quick to see the advantages of European goods, particularly metal. Although trade did take place between the Beothuk and European fishermen, the Beothuk never really had the need to trade to obtain such goods. They could be easily scavenged or pilfered from European fishing locations lying unoccupied during the winter months. Unlike many North American Indian groups, the Beothuk did not move from their casual trade and the stealing and scavenging of European goods in the 1500s, to a coexistant fur trade in the 1600s, but rather withdrew as much as was possible.

As European settlement spread, it appears that the Beothuk increasingly tried to live off coastal resources that were beyond the reach of European economic activity. In the mid-1700s, as the last coastal frontier in inner Notre Dame Bay was frequented by European fur trappers and salmon fishermen, the Beothuk were forced to spend more time in the interior. It also seems likely that European diseases took the same devastating toll on the Beothuk that had earlier been experienced by other Indians, whose contacts had been more frequent with Europeans. This combination of disease and disruption of the traditional seasonal migration probably accounts for the extinction of the Beothuk. However, this is not to say that accounts of the settler savagery in the 1700s ought to be dismissed as a contributing factor.

Of the three cultures to settle Newfoundland and Labrador — Amerindian, Eskimo, and European — each appears to have come in two or more "waves". It seems likely that each was eventually defeated by inadequate supplies of game. The Maritime Archaic, Palaeo-Eskimo, Intermediate Indian and Dorset peoples may either have become extinct when faced with the failure of one or more of the crucial animal resources, or remnant populations were absorbed by more advanced, later migrants. The first wave of Europeans to attempt settlement, the Norse, were apparently unsuccessful because of other factors — perhaps most notably, the hostility of natives, whom they dubbed "Skraelings"— the screechers.

Mi' kmaq women, photographed at Sandy Point, St. George's Bay, in 1859.

On the south and west coasts of Newfoundland, the arrival of the Mi'kmaq may also have played a role in denying the coast to the Beothuk (and paradoxically in the spread of European diseases). It seems most likely that the Mi'kmaq began to come to Newfoundland early in the historic period. They are the only people, to have come to the Island of Newfoundland from the south — across Cabot Strait.

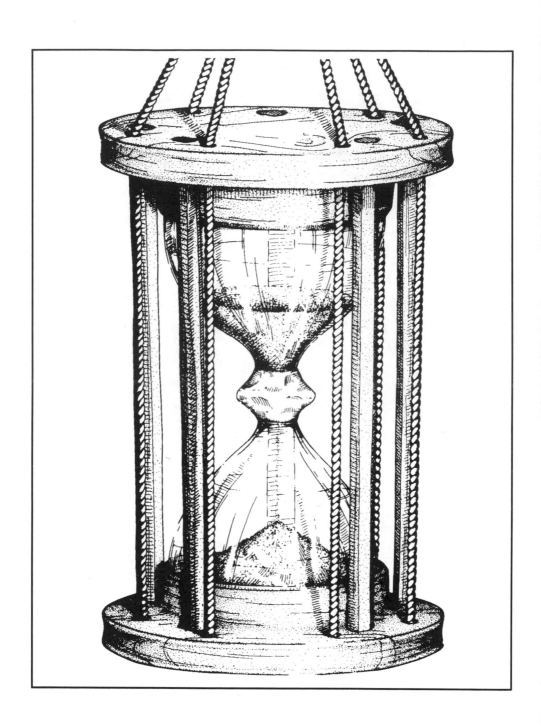

Bibliography.

*Select Bibliography —
Suggested Reading.*

H.P. Biggar. Documents relating to Cartier and Roberval.

H.P. Biggar. *The voyages of the Cabots and of the Corte-Reals to North America and Greenland*, 1497-1503. 1903.

Daniel J. Boorstin. *The discoverers*. 1983.

Fernand Braudel. *The structures of everyday life*. 1981.

J.C. Brevoort. *Verrazzano the navigator*. 1874.

Phillip A. Buckner and John G. Reid eds. *The Atlantic region to confederation: a history*. 1994.

Rebecca Catz. *Christopher Columbus and the Portuguese, 1476-1498*. 1993.

G.T. Cell. *English enterprise in Newfoundland, 1577-1660*. 1969.

Samuel de Champlain. *Works*. 1922-36.

Ramsay Cook ed. *The voyages of Jacques Cartier*. 1993.

W.P. Cumming, R.A. Skelton and D.B. Quinn. *The discovery of North America*. 1972.

Kenneth C. Davis. *Don't know much about geography*. 1992.

Bernard D. Fardy. *John Cabot: the discovery of Newfoundland*. 1994.

Bernard D. Fardy. *Leifsbudir*. 1993.

W.F. Gagnong. *Crucial maps in the early cartography and place-nomenclature of the Atlantic coast of Canada*. 1964.

William H. Guetzman and Glyndwr Williams. *Atlas of North American exploration*. 1992.

Richard Hakluyt. *Divers voyages...*. 1850 ed.

Richard Hakluyt. *Principal navigations*. 1904 ed.

Henry Harrisse. *The discovery of North America*. 1892.

Henry Harrisse. *John Cabot, the discoverer of North America, and Sebastian Cabot his son*. 1896.

B.G. Hoffmann. *Cabot to Cartier*. 1961.

Helge Ingstad. *Westward to Vinland*. 1972.

H.A. Innis. *The Cod Fisheries*. 1954.

Doug Jackson. *"On the country": the Micmac of Newfoundland*. 1993.

Gwyn Jones. *A history of the Vikings*. 1986.

Peter Lacey ed. *Great adventures that changed the world*. 1978

John Latimer.*The history of the Society of Merchant Venturers of the city of Bristol*. 1903.

Jay A. Levenson ed. Circa 1492: *Art in the age of exploration*. 1991.

F.F. Lopes. *The brothers Corte Real*. 1957.

A.G. Macpherson and J.B. Macpherson eds. *The natural environment of Newfoundland past and present*. 1981.

Magnus Magnusson and Hermann Palsson eds. *The Vinland Sagas*. 1975.

P.J. Marshall and Glyndwr Williams. *The great map of mankind*. 1982.

A.H. Markham. *The voyages and works of John Davis, navigator*. 1880.

C.R. Markham. *A life of John Davis, the navigator, 1550-1605*. 1889.

Keith Matthews. *Lectures on the history of Newfoundland, 1500-1830*. 1988.

Robert McGhee. *Ancient Canada*. 1989.

Robert McGhee. *Canada rediscovered*. 1991.

Ingeborg Marshall. *A History and Ethnography of the Beothuk*. 1996.

S.E. Morison. *The European discovery of North America: the northern voyages*. 1971.

S.E. Morison. *The great explorers*. 1978.

S.E. Morison. *Portuguese voyages to America in the fifteenth century*. 1940.

W.A. Munn. *Location of Helluland, Markland and Vinland*. 1929.

W.A. Munn. *Wineland voyages*. 1913.

H.C. Murphy. *The voyage of Verrazzano*. 1875.

Fridtjof Nansen. *In northern mists*. 1911.

Peter Neary and Patrick O'Flaherty. *Part of the main: an illustrated history of Newfoundland and Labrador*. 1983.

Kenneth Nebenzahl. *Maps from the age of discovery*. 1990.

Ralph Pastore. *Shanawdithit's people*. 1992.

Llewellyn Powys. *Henry Hudson*. 1927.

D.W. Prowse. *A history of Newfoundland*. 1895.

Jasper Ridley. *The Tudor Age*, 1988.

D.B. Quinn. "The argument for the English discovery of America between 1480 and 1494", *Geog. Journal*. 1961.

D.B. Quinn et al eds. *The new American world*. 1979.

D.B. Quinn. *North America from earliest discovery to first settlements*. 1977.

D.B. Quinn. *Sir Humphrey Gilbert and Newfoundland*. 1983.

E.R. Seary. *Place names of the Avalon Peninsula of Newfoundland*.

D.R. Stoddart. *On geography and its history*. 1986

G.M. Story ed. *Early European Settlement and Exploitation in Atlantic Canada*. 1982.

E.G.R. Taylor. *Tudor geography, 1485-1583*. 1930.

James A. Tuck. *Newfoundland and Labrador prehistory*. 1976.

W.H. Whiteley. *James Cook in Newfoundland*. 1975.

Alan F. Williams. *John Cabot and Newfoundland*. 1996.

Glyndwr Williams. *The British search for the northwest passage in the eighteenth century.* 1962.

J.A. Williamson. *The Cabot voyages and Bristol discovery under Henry VII.* 1962.

J.A. Williamson. *Voyages of the Cabots.* 1929.

L.C. Wroth. *The voyages of Giovanni da Verrazzano.* 1970.

Dictionary of Canadian Biography. vol. I.

Encyclopedia of Newfoundland and Labrador. vols. I-V.

Newfoundland Studies (Fall 1993, Special Topic Issue: Archaeology in Newfoundland and Labrador)